NYSTCE Family and Consumer Sciences CST

Daisy Z. Fillmore

This page is intentionally left blank.

This page is intentionally left blank.

Table of Content

This page is intentionally left blank.

Chapter 1 – Questions

QUESTION 1

Which of the following factors has the greatest impact on physical development throughout the lifespan?

- A. Genetics
- B. Nutrition
- C. Exercise
- D. Environmental factors

Answer:

QUESTION 2

This question is intentionally removed.

QUESTION 3

What can parents/guardians do to prepare for the addition of a child to the family system?

- A. Establish a strong support network
- B. Buy expensive baby gear
- C. Ignore the changes and continue with their current lifestyle
- D. Avoid seeking professional help

Answer:

QUESTION 4

According to Kubler-Ross's stages of grief, which stage involves a period of bargaining?

- A. Denial
- B. Anger
- C. Bargaining
- D. Depression

Answer:

QUESTION 5

When should parents begin talking to their children about sexuality and relationships?

- A. In early childhood
- B. In adolescence
- C. When the child begins dating
- D. When the child expresses interest or asks questions

Answer:

QUESTION 6

Which of the following is an example of a blended family?

    A. A family consisting of a married couple and their children
    B. A family consisting of a single parent and their child
    C. A family consisting of a divorced parent and their child, and a remarried parent and their child
    D. A family consisting of grandparents raising their grandchildren

Answer:

QUESTION7

During which trimester of pregnancy does the majority of fetal development occur?

    A. First trimester
    B. Second trimester
    C. Third trimester
    D. It is evenly spread out across all three trimesters

Answer:

QUESTION 8

Which of the following is a key factor in emotional development throughout the lifespan?

    A. Genetics
    B. Socioeconomic status
    C. Education level
    D. Nutrition

Answer:

QUESTION 9

This question is intentionally removed.

QUESTION 10

According to research, what are some of the benefits of family mealtime and how can families make mealtime more enjoyable and successful?

    A. Benefits include improved nutrition, better communication, and enhanced family relationships; families can make mealtime more enjoyable and successful by involving children in meal planning and preparation, setting a positive and relaxed atmosphere, and limiting distractions such as technology.
    B. Benefits include increased physical activity, improved academic performance, and decreased risk of substance abuse; families can make mealtime more enjoyable and successful by providing a variety of foods and encouraging conversation and positive interactions.
    C. Benefits include improved mental health, increased self-esteem, and decreased risk of chronic diseases; families can make mealtime more enjoyable and successful by implementing strict rules and consequences, focusing on healthy eating habits, and discouraging picky eating.
    D. Benefits include improved social skills, better sleep patterns, and enhanced cognitive development; families can make mealtime more enjoyable and successful by setting a consistent mealtime schedule, involving extended family members, and prioritizing the importance of family mealtime.

Answer:

QUESTION 11

According to Maslow's hierarchy of needs, which of the following needs must be met before one can move on to self-actualization?

    A.   Safety needs
    B.   Esteem needs
    C.   Love and belonging needs
    D.   Physiological needs

Answer:

QUESTION 12

Which of the following is a responsibility of family members?

    A.   Providing financial support
    B.   Providing emotional support
    C.   Providing healthcare services
    D.   Providing job opportunities

Answer:

QUESTION 13

Sarah is a 12-year-old girl who is struggling in school and has become increasingly withdrawn from her family and friends. Her parents are concerned about her emotional development and are looking for ways to support her. Which of the following strategies would be most effective in supporting Sarah's emotional development?

    A.   Enrolling her in an academic tutoring program
    B.   Encouraging her to join a sports team
    C.   Setting aside regular one-on-one time with her parents
    D.   Telling her to focus on getting better grades

Answer:

QUESTION 14

What strategies can individuals use to effectively manage crises and minimize their impact?

    A.   Prepare in advance by creating a crisis management plan and practicing emergency response procedures.
    B.   Communicate clearly and frequently with those affected by the crisis, providing accurate information and updates.
    C.   Prioritize the safety and well-being of individuals and communities, and provide support to those who are affected.
    D.   Address the root causes of the crisis and work to prevent similar crises from occurring in the future.

Answer:

QUESTION 15

Which of the following is an example of a developmentally appropriate strategy for promoting children's social development?

    A.   Forcing children to share their toys and belongings with others
    B.   Encouraging children to make their own decisions without guidance or support
    C.   Providing opportunities for cooperative play and group activities
    D.   Criticizing or belittling children for social mistakes or misbehavior

Answer:

QUESTION 16

Which of the following is NOT a common challenge faced by parents?

    A. Balancing work and family responsibilities
    B. Dealing with their own emotional reactions to their children's behavior
    C. Communicating effectively with their children
    D. Having too much free time on their hands

Answer:

QUESTION 17

Which of the following is an important resource for fostering optimal physical, emotional, social, and cognitive development?

    A. Access to social media and technology
    B. Access to high-calorie and sugary snacks
    C. Access to safe and supportive environments
    D. Access to violent or graphic media content

Answer:

QUESTION 18

How can families with children with special needs navigate the challenges of accessing appropriate services and support, and what resources are available to help them?

    A. Special education advocacy groups and legal resources
    B. General education curriculum and mainstreaming programs
    C. Private tutoring and specialized therapy services
    D. Community support groups and disability organizations

Answer:

QUESTION 19

Which of the following is a characteristic of a healthy interpersonal relationship?

    A. A lack of communication
    B. A focus on power dynamics
    C. Mutual respect and trust
    D. A lack of empathy

Answer:

QUESTION 20

A student in your class is struggling with personal issues that are affecting their academic performance. As their teacher, what should you do?

    A. Ignore the situation and focus only on their academic performance.
    B. Encourage the student to handle their personal issues on their own.
    C. Offer support and resources to help the student address their personal issues and improve their academic performance.
    D. Punish the student for poor academic performance.

Answer:

QUESTION 21

A parent expresses concerns that her child is not meeting developmental milestones and seems to be falling behind in their physical and cognitive development. Which of the following strategies would be most appropriate for promoting the child's development?

    A. Giving the child more screen time to keep them occupied
    B. Encouraging the child to engage in physical activities like sports or dance
    C. Allowing the child to skip meals to focus on academic progress
    D. Focusing solely on academic progress and neglecting physical and social development

Answer:

QUESTION 22

Sarah is a new mother who is concerned about her infant son's development. She asks her pediatrician for advice on how to promote her son's cognitive and social development. What is the best resource for the pediatrician to recommend?

    A. A social media group for new parents
    B. A children's television program
    C. A community playgroup or parent-child class
    D. A video game or smartphone app

Answer:

QUESTION 23

A student in your classroom has a severe allergic reaction during lunch. What should you do first?

    A. Call 911
    B. Administer the student's epinephrine auto-injector
    C. Take the student to the school nurse's office
    D. Have another student bring the student to the school office

Answer:

QUESTION 24

Which of the following is an important benefit of interpersonal relationships for well-being?

    A. Increased stress and anxiety
    B. Improved physical health
    C. Decreased social support
    D. Decreased sense of belonging

Answer:

QUESTION 25

A teacher is working with a student who has a learning disability and is struggling to keep up with their peers in class. Which of the following strategies would be most appropriate for promoting the student's academic development?

    A. Giving the student less challenging assignments to complete
    B. Providing the student with extra support and resources, such as tutoring or assistive technology
    C. Expecting the student to keep up with their peers without any additional support
    D. Ignoring the student's academic difficulties and focusing on social skills development

Answer:

QUESTION 26

What are some of the common challenges faced by single parents, and which of the following support systems can be most helpful in assisting single parents in meeting these challenges?

    A. Family and friends who can provide emotional support and assistance with childcare
    B. Government-sponsored programs that offer financial assistance and job training
    C. Community-based organizations that provide parenting classes and workshops
    D. Faith-based organizations that offer counseling and spiritual guidance

Answer:

QUESTION 27

How can families best manage conflict and crisis within the family unit?

    A. By avoiding conflict at all costs
    B. By engaging in healthy conflict resolution strategies
    C. By blaming others for the problem
    D. By refusing to acknowledge that there is a problem

Answer:

QUESTION 28

Which of the following is a characteristic of the sensorimotor stage of development, according to Piaget's theory of cognitive development?

    A. Abstract reasoning
    B. Object permanence
    C. Formal operations
    D. Conservation

Answer:

QUESTION 29

Which of the following is an example of a non-normative life event?

    A. Graduating from college
    B. Getting married
    C. Losing a limb
    D. Retiring from work

Answer:

QUESTION 30

What is the term for a parenting style that involves warmth, affection, clear rules and consequences, and open communication?

    A. Authoritarian
    B. Permissive
    C. Authoritative
    D. Uninvolved

Answer:

QUESTION 31

Which of the following is an effective communication skill that can improve relationships?

    A. Interrupting others when they are speaking
    B. Criticizing or blaming others for their mistakes
    C. Using "I" statements to express one's feelings and needs
    D. Ignoring the emotions of others and focusing solely on facts

Answer:

QUESTION 32

How can community involvement benefit personal and family roles and responsibilities?

    A. It has no impact on personal and family roles and responsibilities
    B. It can create a sense of purpose and fulfillment
    C. It can lead to neglect of personal and family roles and responsibilities
    D. It can create conflict and tension in personal and family relationships

Answer:

QUESTION 33

Which of the following is an example of a nonverbal communication cue?

    A. Speaking loudly
    B. Nodding
    C. Interrupting
    D. Using complex language

Answer:

QUESTION 34

This question is intentionally removed.

QUESTION 35

What is the primary goal of parenting?

    A. To make sure the child is always happy
    B. To provide the child with everything they want
    C. To help the child become a responsible and independent adult
    D. To control the child's behavior

Answer:

QUESTION 36

Jean Piaget's cognitive development theory consists of which four stages?

    A. Sensorimotor, Preoperational, Concrete Operational, Formal Operational
    B. Identity, Intimacy, Generativity, Ego Integrity
    C. Trust vs. Mistrust, Autonomy vs. Shame and Doubt, Initiative vs. Guilt, Industry vs. Inferiority
    D. Oral, Anal, Phallic, Latency

Answer:

QUESTION 37

Which of the following is NOT a factor that can affect parenting styles, expectations, and responsibilities?

- A. Cultural background
- B. Family values
- C. Socioeconomic status
- D. Hair color

Answer:

QUESTION 38

What are some potential consequences of poverty on families and children?

- A. Limited access to resources, poor health outcomes, and educational challenges
- B. Increased social support, better family cohesion, and enhanced creativity
- C. Improved mental health, increased access to healthcare, and better job opportunities
- D. Stronger family ties, increased opportunities for social mobility, and improved overall well-being

Answer:

QUESTION 39

In a command economy, the government makes all economic decisions and allocates resources. How does this impact consumer behavior?

- A. Consumers are free to purchase any goods or services they want.
- B. Consumers have no influence over the production or allocation of goods and services.
- C. Consumers are required to purchase goods and services based on government regulations.
- D. Consumers are able to choose which businesses receive government subsidies.

Answer:

QUESTION 40

What is the most important thing parents can do to keep their child safe?

- A. Keeping the child under constant surveillance
- B. Teaching the child to be cautious and wary of strangers
- C. Keeping potentially dangerous items out of the child's reach
- D. Ignoring potential safety hazards

Answer:

QUESTION 41

Mrs. Rodriguez, a preschool teacher, notices that one of her students seems to have difficulty forming attachments to caregivers and often seems indifferent to adults. According to Mary Ainsworth's attachment theory, which attachment style might this child be exhibiting?

- A. Secure attachment
- B. Anxious-ambivalent attachment
- C. Avoidant attachment
- D. Disorganized attachment

Answer:

QUESTION 42

What are some factors that may influence a parent's choice of parenting style?

    A.   Cultural background, personal values, and child's temperament
    B.   Income level, marital status, and child's age
    C.   Education level, geographical location, and child's gender
    D.   Religious beliefs, job status, and child's hobbies

Answer:

QUESTION 43

What is the primary factor that affects family well-being?

    A.   Income
    B.   Number of children
    C.   Marital status
    D.   Ethnicity

Answer:

QUESTION 44

Which of the following businesses typically provides loans for higher education?

    A.   Credit card companies
    B.   Mortgage lenders
    C.   Payday loan centers
    D.   Student loan servicers

Answer:

QUESTION 45

What is the difference between a need and a want, and why is it important to distinguish between the two?

    A.   A need is something that is essential for survival, while a want is something that is desired but not necessary. It is important to distinguish between the two because prioritizing needs over wants can help individuals and families make wise financial decisions.
    B.   A need is something that is desired but not necessary, while a want is something that is essential for survival. It is important to distinguish between the two because prioritizing wants over needs can lead to financial hardship.
    C.   A need and a want are the same thing, and there is no difference between the two. It is not important to distinguish between the two because they both serve the same purpose.
    D.   A need and a want are both subjective terms, and the distinction between the two can vary depending on the individual. It is important to understand each individual's definition of need and want in order to make informed financial decisions.

Answer:

QUESTION 46

According to Lev Vygotsky's sociocultural theory, what is the role of language in cognitive development and how does it differ from Jean Piaget's cognitive development theory?

- A. Language is a tool for thinking and learning, and plays a central role in cognitive development. In Piaget's theory, language development is seen as a byproduct of cognitive development, rather than a critical component.
- B. Language development occurs independently of cognitive development, and is primarily determined by environmental factors such as exposure and reinforcement. In Piaget's theory, language development is seen as a precursor to cognitive development.
- C. Language is a product of cognitive development, and is primarily determined by biological factors such as brain maturation. In Piaget's theory, language development and cognitive development are seen as closely intertwined.
- D. Language is a passive receiver of cognitive development, and has little impact on the overall development of cognitive abilities. In Piaget's theory, language development is seen as a secondary aspect of cognitive development.

Answer:

QUESTION 47

According to the nature vs. nurture debate, which of the following best describes the role of genetics in shaping an individual's needs, roles, and goals?

- A. Genetics play a dominant role in shaping an individual's needs, roles, and goals, with little influence from environmental factors.
- B. Environmental factors play a dominant role in shaping an individual's needs, roles, and goals, with little influence from genetic factors.
- C. Genetics and environmental factors both play a role in shaping an individual's needs, roles, and goals, with the relative influence of each varying depending on the trait or characteristic in question.
- D. Genetics and environmental factors do not play a significant role in shaping an individual's needs, roles, and goals, which are largely determined by personal choice and socialization.

Answer:

QUESTION 48

What are some of the signs of child neglect?

- A. Unexplained bruises and injuries
- B. Poor hygiene
- C. Sudden changes in behavior
- D. All of the above

Answer:

QUESTION 49

Jessica is a single mother of two children who recently lost her job. She needs financial assistance to cover her rent and utilities while she searches for a new job. Which agency should she contact for assistance?

- A. Internal Revenue Service (IRS)
- B. Federal Deposit Insurance Corporation (FDIC)
- C. Social Security Administration (SSA)
- D. Department of Housing and Urban Development (HUD)

Answer:

QUESTION 50

When making purchasing decisions, what is an example of an external influence?

    A. Personal values and beliefs
    B. Income level and financial resources
    C. Peer pressure and social norms
    D. Prior experiences and knowledge

Answer:

QUESTION 51

Which of the following is an important consideration when selecting furnishings and equipment for a home?

    A. Durability
    B. Brand popularity
    C. Color coordination
    D. Price point

Answer:

QUESTION 52

What is the definition of a budget?

    A. A plan for spending and saving money
    B. A list of expenses from the previous month
    C. A record of all financial transactions
    D. A summary of a person's net worth

Answer:

QUESTION 53

Maria is considering applying for a credit card but is unsure of what factors affect her eligibility for credit. Which of the following factors is most likely to affect her eligibility for credit?

    A. Her employment status and income
    B. Her age and gender
    C. Her race and ethnicity
    D. Her level of education and occupation

Answer:

QUESTION 54

Juanita is planning to buy a new laptop for her college studies. She has a budget of $800 and is looking for a laptop that is lightweight, has a long battery life, and can handle graphic design software. She starts her research online by visiting different e-commerce websites and reading reviews. Which of the following is an example of a secondary source of information that Juanita could use to aid in her decision-making process?

    A. A laptop review blog written by a tech enthusiast
    B. A laptop review video made by a popular YouTuber
    C. The official website of the laptop manufacturer
    D. The laptop product page on an e-commerce website

Answer:

QUESTION 55

You are trying to decide whether to lease or buy a new car. Which of the following is a disadvantage of leasing a car?

    A.   You have to make a large down payment
    B.   You have to pay for maintenance and repairs
    C.   You have to return the car at the end of the lease
    D.   You have to pay higher monthly payments than when buying a car

Answer:

QUESTION 56

Which of the following is a consideration when selecting furniture for a family room?

    A.   The size of the furniture relative to the size of the room
    B.   The style and color of the furniture
    C.   The durability of the material
    D.   The price of the furniture compared to other options

Answer:

QUESTION 57

What is the difference between a savings account and a checking account?

    A.   Savings accounts earn interest, while checking accounts do not
    B.   Savings accounts have higher fees than checking accounts
    C.   Savings accounts allow unlimited withdrawals, while checking accounts do not
    D.   Savings accounts are used for short-term savings, while checking accounts are used for long-term savings

Answer:

QUESTION 58

Which of the following is an example of adjusting a resource to meet a changing circumstance?

    A.   Continuing to drive a car with a flat tire
    B.   Ignoring a leaky faucet and letting it waste water
    C.   Buying a smaller home when your children move out
    D.   Keeping a large home despite financial difficulties

Answer:

QUESTION 59

Maria is in the market for a new smartphone and is considering two models: Model A and Model B. Model A has a larger screen and longer battery life but is more expensive than Model B. Model B, on the other hand, has a faster processor and a better camera but has a smaller screen and shorter battery life. Maria is having a hard time deciding between the two models as she values both features equally. Which of the following decision-making strategies can Maria use to make a decision?

    A.   Satisficing
    B.   Intuition
    C.   Heuristics
    D.   Anchoring and adjustment

Answer:

QUESTION 60

You are considering taking out a mortgage to purchase a home. Which of the following is a disadvantage of a fixed-rate mortgage?

A. The interest rate may change over time
B. You may have to pay a higher interest rate than with an adjustable-rate mortgage
C. You may have to pay a penalty for prepaying the mortgage
D. You may have to pay higher monthly payments than with an adjustable-rate mortgage

Answer:

QUESTION 61

Which of the following factors can affect an individual's money management and financial planning in the short-term?

A. Age
B. Job security
C. Homeownership
D. Political affiliation

Answer:

QUESTION 62

Sarah is a single mother of two who recently lost her job. She is struggling to make ends meet and pay her bills. Which strategy could Sarah use to adapt her resources to meet her needs?

A. Selling her car and using public transportation
B. Ignoring her bills and hoping for the best
C. Borrowing money from payday lenders
D. Continuing to use her credit cards to make purchases

Answer:

QUESTION 63

Which federal agency is responsible for enforcing laws related to food safety?

A. Environmental Protection Agency (EPA)
B. Food and Drug Administration (FDA)
C. Consumer Product Safety Commission (CPSC)
D. Federal Trade Commission (FTC)

Answer:

QUESTION 64

What is a step involved in developing a budget?

A. Increase your debt
B. Spend more money than you earn
C. Prioritize your expenses
D. Ignore your financial situation

Answer:

QUESTION 65

What is the purpose of insurance?

    A. To protect against financial losses
    B. To increase debt
    C. To restrict spending
    D. To decrease savings

Answer:

QUESTION 66

What is the difference between fixed and variable expenses when creating a budget?

    A. Fixed expenses are one-time costs while variable expenses are recurring costs
    B. Fixed expenses stay the same while variable expenses change over time
    C. Fixed expenses can be easily reduced while variable expenses cannot
    D. Fixed expenses are unnecessary while variable expenses are essential

Answer:

QUESTION 67

What is a characteristic of a traditional Individual Retirement Account (IRA)?

    A. Contributions are tax-deductible
    B. Contributions are taxed when withdrawn
    C. Anyone can contribute regardless of income
    D. Contributions are not limited by the government

Answer:

QUESTION 68

You are looking to reduce your water usage at home. Which of the following practices would be the most effective in conserving water?

    A. Taking long showers and using a high-flow showerhead
    B. Running the dishwasher with only a few dishes
    C. Watering your lawn every day
    D. Installing low-flow faucets and showerheads

Answer:

QUESTION 69

Which of the following fabrics is known for its durability and is commonly used in outdoor clothing and equipment?

    A. Polyester
    B. Cotton
    C. Wool
    D. Silk

Answer:

QUESTION 70

What is the role of proteins in food science?

    A. To provide energy
    B. To add flavor
    C. To promote browning
    D. To provide structure and texture

Answer:

QUESTION 71

Which of the following is a potential complication of untreated celiac disease?

    A. Iron deficiency anemia
    B. Hypertension
    C. Osteoarthritis
    D. Asthma

Answer:

QUESTION 72

Which of the following is an example of consumer fraud?

    A. A company offering a legitimate product at a higher price than its competitors
    B. A company falsely claiming that their product can cure a disease
    C. A company using aggressive marketing techniques to sell a product
    D. A company selling expired products at a discounted price

Answer:

QUESTION 73

What is a characteristic of synthetic fibers, such as polyester or nylon, that make them popular for use in outdoor apparel?

    A. They are lightweight and breathable, allowing for ease of movement and comfort during physical activity.
    B. They are moisture-wicking, which means they can pull sweat away from the body and keep the wearer dry.
    C. They are resistant to wrinkles, making them ideal for travel or storage.
    D. They are naturally hypoallergenic, reducing the risk of skin irritation or allergic reactions.

Answer:

QUESTION 74

What are the four types of heat transfer, and which type of heat transfer occurs when cooking food in a pot of boiling water?

    A. Conduction, convection, radiation, and induction; convection
    B. Conduction, convection, radiation, and induction; conduction
    C. Radiation, convection, induction, and conduction; radiation
    D. Radiation, convection, induction, and conduction; convection

Answer:

QUESTION 75

Which of the following environmental factors can affect food safety?

    A. Temperature
    B. Soil pH
    C. Wind speed
    D. Water pressure

Answer:

QUESTION 76

Jack received a phone call from a person claiming to be from his bank and asking for his personal information, including his Social Security number and account password. The caller told Jack that his account was compromised and needed immediate action to prevent unauthorized access. What should Jack do?

    A. Provide the information requested by the caller to protect his account
    B. Hang up the phone and contact his bank directly using a trusted phone number
    C. Follow the instructions provided by the caller to secure his account
    D. Report the call to the police

Answer:

QUESTION 77

What is a characteristic of cotton fabric that makes it a good choice for warm weather clothing?

    A. It is moisture-wicking, which helps keep the wearer dry and comfortable.
    B. It is insulating, which helps regulate body temperature in cooler weather.
    C. It is naturally flame-resistant, providing added safety in case of fire.
    D. It is lightweight and breathable, allowing for ease of movement and comfort in hot weather.

Answer:

QUESTION 78

Which of the following claims on a food label must meet specific criteria set by the FDA?

    A. "Natural"
    B. "Organic"
    C. "Low-fat"
    D. "Made with whole grains"

Answer:

QUESTION 79

What does the "Percent Daily Value" (%DV) on a food label indicate?

    A. The percentage of the recommended daily intake for each nutrient provided by one serving of the food
    B. The percentage of the total daily calorie intake that should come from each macronutrient
    C. The percentage of the recommended daily intake for each nutrient provided by the entire package or container of food
    D. The percentage of the total daily calorie intake that should come from added sugars

Answer:

QUESTION 80

You are preparing a meal for your family and realize that you left the chicken out of the refrigerator for several hours. What should you do?

A. Wash the chicken thoroughly with hot water and cook it immediately
B. Discard the chicken and choose a different protein source for the meal
C. Freeze the chicken and use it for a future meal
D. Cook the chicken at a higher temperature to ensure any bacteria is killed

Answer:

QUESTION 81

Tom is a chef at a restaurant that is introducing a new menu. He wants to ensure that the pricing of the dishes is appropriate to cover the cost of ingredients and other expenses while still being competitive. Which of the following pricing strategies would be the most effective for Tom to use?

A. Markup pricing
B. Cost-plus pricing
C. Competition-based pricing
D. Skimming pricing

Answer:

QUESTION 82

Sarah is planning a dinner party for eight people and wants to create a three-course meal within a budget of $100. She has decided on a menu but realizes that she is over budget. Which of the following would be the most effective way for Sarah to reduce costs while still providing a satisfying meal for her guests?

A. Reduce the portion sizes of each dish
B. Switch to lower quality ingredients
C. Remove one course from the menu
D. Eliminate the dessert course

Answer:

QUESTION 83

Maria is a single parent who works full-time and also cares for her elderly mother. She is feeling burned out and stressed, and doesn't know how to manage all of her responsibilities. What is a potential strategy that Maria can use to manage her personal and family commitments?

A. Ignoring her own self-care needs to focus on her mother and work responsibilities.
B. Asking her children to take on more caregiving responsibilities.
C. Setting aside dedicated time each week for self-care activities.
D. Prioritizing work responsibilities over personal and family commitments.

Answer:

QUESTION 84

Which of the following is a special nutritional need for pregnant women, and is important for the development of the baby's brain and nervous system?

A. Iron
B. Vitamin C
C. Folic acid
D. Calcium

Answer:

QUESTION 85

What should you do in case of a kitchen emergency?

- A. Call a friend
- B. Evacuate the building immediately
- C. Put out the fire using water
- D. Use a fire extinguisher

Answer:

QUESTION 86

Which of the following is a common kitchen safety hazard related to food handling?

- A. Keeping raw meat at room temperature for several hours
- B. Using a sharp knife to cut vegetables
- C. Washing fruits and vegetables thoroughly before eating them
- D. Storing dry goods in airtight containers

Answer:

QUESTION 87

Which of the following is an example of a low-glycemic index food?

- A. White bread
- B. Brown rice
- C. Watermelon
- D. Instant oatmeal

Answer:

QUESTION 88

Which of the following should be done before handling food?

- A. Washing hands with soap and warm water for at least 20 seconds
- B. Using hand sanitizer
- C. Wiping hands on a towel
- D. None of the above

Answer:

QUESTION 89

Which of the following is a principle of healthy eating?

- A. Avoiding all fats
- B. Eliminating carbohydrates from the diet
- C. Eating a variety of foods
- D. Consuming only organic foods

Answer:

QUESTION 90

Which of the following is a factor that can affect food choices, food customs, and eating habits?

    A.   Income level
    B.   Hair color
    C.   Favorite TV show
    D.   Height

Answer:

QUESTION 91

What is the most effective method for preventing cross-contamination in a commercial kitchen?

    A.   Using separate cutting boards for different types of food
    B.   Washing hands frequently and thoroughly
    C.   Keeping raw meat and ready-to-eat foods separate
    D.   Using gloves when handling food

Answer:

QUESTION 92

Which of the following is a meal service style that is common in formal dining events?

    A.   Buffet service
    B.   Family-style service
    C.   Plated service
    D.   Cafeteria-style service

Answer:

QUESTION 93

Jenny is making a cake and realizes that she doesn't have a hand mixer to cream the butter and sugar together. She decides to use a blender instead. What is the likely result of this decision?

    A.   The cake will turn out perfectly.
    B.   The cake will be over-mixed and dense.
    C.   The cake will not rise properly.
    D.   The cake will have a strange texture and flavor.

Answer:

QUESTION 94

What is the role of food advertising in shaping food choices and dietary habits?

    A.   Food advertising has no impact on food choices or dietary habits.
    B.   Food advertising can promote healthy food choices and dietary habits.
    C.   Food advertising can promote unhealthy food choices and dietary habits.
    D.   Food advertising has a minimal impact on food choices and dietary habits.

Answer:

QUESTION 95

How does genetic modification of crops affect their nutrient content?

    A. Genetic modification can increase the nutrient content of crops, such as by adding vitamins

    B. Genetic modification has no effect on the nutrient content of crops

    C. Genetic modification can decrease the nutrient content of crops, such as by reducing the protein content

    D. Genetic modification can only affect the appearance, not the nutrient content, of crops

Answer:

QUESTION 96

Which of the following is a recommended technique for promoting healthy eating habits in workplaces?

    A. Providing only healthy food options in vending machines and break rooms

    B. Mandating that all employees bring their own lunch from home

    C. Offering free junk food and soda to employees as a perk

    D. Having regular healthy potlucks and cooking demonstrations

Answer:

QUESTION 97

Which of the following is an example of a healthy food choice for someone with high blood pressure?

    A. Bacon cheeseburger

    B. Grilled salmon with quinoa and roasted vegetables

    C. Fried chicken with mashed potatoes and gravy

    D. Pepperoni pizza

Answer:

QUESTION 98

Which of the following skills is most important for a career in family and consumer sciences?

    A. Strong written communication skills

    B. Advanced math skills

    C. Ability to work independently

    D. Attention to detail

Answer:

QUESTION 99

Which of the following work experiences is most relevant for a career in nutrition and dietetics?

    A. Experience working in a retail store

    B. Experience in the hospitality industry

    C. Experience working in a hospital or healthcare setting

    D. Experience in a manufacturing facility

Answer:

QUESTION 100

You have a customer who is interested in taking a sewing class at your family and consumer sciences program, but they are hesitant because they have never sewn before. How can you address their concerns and build a strong relationship with them?

A. Suggest that they take a different class that may be more suitable for their level of experience
B. Offer to provide additional support and guidance during the class
C. Tell them that they will be fine and that sewing is easy to learn
D. Encourage them to bring a friend or family member to the class for support

Answer:

QUESTION 101

Which of the following is an example of a career opportunity related to family and consumer sciences professions?

A. Chef
B. Mechanical Engineer
C. Lawyer
D. Architect

Answer:

QUESTION 102

This question is intentionally removed.

QUESTION 103

Which of the following ethical behaviors is important for success in leadership?

A. Lack of accountability and responsibility
B. Honesty and integrity
C. Manipulative behavior
D. Favoritism and bias

Answer:

QUESTION 104

A fashion design graduate is interested in pursuing a career in sustainable fashion. What would be the best strategy to break into this field?

A. Start their own eco-friendly clothing line
B. Apply for a job at a well-established sustainable fashion company
C. Volunteer for a nonprofit organization that promotes sustainable fashion practices
D. Attend trade shows and networking events to connect with other sustainable fashion professionals

Answer:

QUESTION 105

This question is intentionally removed.

QUESTION 106

What are the qualities that employers often look for when hiring new employees?

    A.   Good physical fitness and health
    B.   Advanced technical skills
    C.   Positive attitude and good work ethic
    D.   Fluency in multiple languages

Answer:

QUESTION 107

Which of the following methods can be used for exploring career opportunities in Family and Consumer Sciences?

    A.   Researching job descriptions and requirements
    B.   Conducting informational interviews with professionals in the field
    C.   Participating in job shadowing or internships
    D.   All of the above

Answer:

QUESTION 108

Which of the following best describes the current employment trend in family and consumer sciences career paths?

    A.   A decline in employment opportunities due to automation and outsourcing of jobs.
    B.   A steady increase in demand for professionals with expertise in technology and design.
    C.   A shift towards entrepreneurship and self-employment opportunities in the field.
    D.   An increase in demand for professionals with expertise in sustainable living and green technology.

Answer:

QUESTION 109

When applying for a job, which of the following steps is NOT necessary?

    A.   Researching the company and the position
    B.   Tailoring your resume and cover letter to the job posting
    C.   Following up with the employer after submitting your application
    D.   Submitting multiple applications to increase your chances of getting hired

Answer:

QUESTION 110

According to the Americans with Disabilities Act (ADA), what are the requirements for accessibility in public accommodations for individuals with disabilities?

    A.   Only new construction projects must comply with accessibility requirements.
    B.   Public accommodations are not required to remove barriers to accessibility if it is too expensive.
    C.   Public accommodations must remove existing barriers to accessibility if it is readily achievable to do so.
    D.   Only state and local government agencies are required to comply with accessibility requirements.

Answer:

QUESTION 111

Your new job in a family and consumer science organization requires you to manage a team of employees. You have noticed that one of your team members is consistently missing deadlines and not completing their work to the expected level of quality. What is the best course of action for you as their manager?

    A.   Fire the employee immediately to set an example for the rest of the team.
    B.   Confront the employee in a public setting to show that their behavior is unacceptable.
    C.   Schedule a private meeting with the employee to discuss the issues and develop a plan for improvement.
    D.   Ignore the issue and hope that it resolves itself over time.

Answer:

QUESTION 112

Which of the following professions is an example of a career opportunity in the field of family and consumer sciences?

    A.   Civil Engineer
    B.   Personal Trainer
    C.   Biomedical Scientist
    D.   Aerospace Technician

Answer:

QUESTION 113

You are a family and consumer sciences teacher who has been tasked with teaching financial literacy to your students. Which of the following strategies would be most effective for promoting financial responsibility?

    A.   Encouraging students to use credit cards for everyday purchases
    B.   Demonstrating how to budget for short-term goals only
    C.   Discussing the consequences of debt and strategies for debt management
    D.   Promoting impulse buying and immediate gratification

Answer:

QUESTION 114

What is the purpose of FCCLA?

    A.   To provide students with opportunities to develop leadership and communication skills
    B.   To provide students with opportunities to learn about different career paths
    C.   To provide students with opportunities to socialize with peers
    D.   To provide students with opportunities to earn money

Answer:

QUESTION 115

Which of the following ethical behaviors is important for success in the workplace?

    A.   Dishonesty
    B.   Transparency
    C.   Lack of accountability
    D.   Disrespect

Answer:

QUESTION 116

Which of the following strategies can foster optimal physical, emotional, social, and cognitive development from early childhood throughout the life span?

    A. Encouraging children to spend long hours watching TV or playing video games
    B. Providing children with opportunities for regular physical activity and exercise
    C. Criticizing and shaming children for their mistakes and failures
    D. Allowing children to consume unhealthy food and sugary drinks

Answer:

QUESTION 117

A family is experiencing a crisis as a result of a natural disaster that has destroyed their home. What is a resource that could help them during this time?

    A. The Federal Emergency Management Agency (FEMA) provides disaster assistance to families in need. This may include financial assistance for temporary housing, home repairs, and other disaster-related expenses.
    B. The American Red Cross provides emergency shelter, food, and emotional support to families affected by natural disasters. They may also provide financial assistance to help families get back on their feet.
    C. The Salvation Army provides disaster relief services to families in need. This may include emergency shelter, food, and other basic needs. They may also provide financial assistance to help families recover from the disaster.
    D. Local churches and community organizations often provide support and resources to families affected by natural disasters. They may offer temporary housing, food, and other basic needs, as well as emotional support and counseling.

Answer:

QUESTION 118

What is the role of parents in promoting the physical health and well-being of their children, and which of the following strategies would be most effective for parents to use when encouraging their children to adopt healthy habits?

    A. Setting a good example by modeling healthy behaviors themselves
    B. Enrolling their children in extracurricular activities that promote physical activity
    C. Monitoring their children's diets and limiting their access to unhealthy foods and beverages
    D. Punishing their children for engaging in unhealthy behaviors, such as eating junk food or skipping exercise

Answer:

QUESTION 119

Which of the following is a skill that is necessary for building and maintaining healthy family relationships?

    A. Avoiding conflict and confrontation
    B. Communicating effectively
    C. Putting individual needs above the needs of the family
    D. Refusing to compromise on important issues

Answer:

QUESTION 120

Sarah is a new mom who is struggling to maintain a healthy environment for her baby at home. She is unsure about how to properly store breastmilk and how often to wash her baby's bottles. What advice should you give Sarah?

A. "You should always wash your baby's bottles after every use and store breastmilk in the refrigerator for up to 72 hours."
B. "You should always wash your baby's bottles after every use and store breastmilk in the freezer for up to 3 months."
C. "You should wash your baby's bottles every few uses and store breastmilk in the refrigerator for up to 48 hours."
D. "You should wash your baby's bottles every few uses and store breastmilk in the freezer for up to 6 months."

Answer:

QUESTION 121

A group of students in your class are not getting along with each other and there have been several instances of conflict between them. As their teacher, what is the best course of action?

A. Ignore the situation as it is not affecting their academic performance.
B. Call the students' parents and ask them to handle the situation.
C. Bring the students together and facilitate a discussion to understand the root cause of the conflict and find a solution.
D. Suspend the students who are causing the conflict to set an example for others.

Answer:

QUESTION 122

Which of the following is a factor that may affect a person's decision about becoming a parent/guardian?

A. Financial stability and resources
B. Gender identity
C. Height and weight
D. Favorite color

Answer:

QUESTION 123

What is the best way for parents to support their child's academic success?

A. Providing tutoring or academic support services
B. Encouraging extracurricular activities
C. Setting high expectations for academic performance
D. All of the above

Answer:

QUESTION 124

Which of the following is a key responsibility of parents when it comes to their children's education?

A. Ensuring that their children attend school regularly
B. Helping with homework and projects
C. Encouraging their children to pursue extracurricular activities
D. All of the above

Answer:

QUESTION 125

Which of the following is an example of a communication barrier that can negatively affect relationships?

    A. Interrupting the speaker and not allowing them to finish their thoughts and ideas

    B. Criticizing the speaker and making personal attacks

    C. Using open-ended questions to encourage the speaker to elaborate on their ideas

    D. Engaging in active listening and paraphrasing the speaker's message to confirm understanding

Answer:

QUESTION 126

How does consumer behavior impact the U.S. economy?

    A. Consumer behavior has no impact on the U.S. economy.

    B. Consumer behavior can influence production and employment levels, which impact the U.S. economy.

    C. Consumer behavior only impacts local economies, not the U.S. economy as a whole.

    D. Consumer behavior can lead to economic growth or recession, depending on the level of demand for goods and services.

Answer:

QUESTION 127

According to Erik Erikson's theory of psychosocial development, which stage occurs during adolescence and what is the primary crisis or challenge that individuals face during this stage?

    A. Identity vs. Role Confusion, in which individuals are tasked with developing a sense of self and a clear identity, or risk confusion about their place in the world.

    B. Generativity vs. Stagnation, in which individuals are tasked with contributing to society and making a positive impact, or risk feeling unfulfilled and stagnant in their personal growth.

    C. Intimacy vs. Isolation, in which individuals are tasked with forming close, meaningful relationships with others, or risk feeling isolated and alone.

    D. Industry vs. Inferiority, in which individuals are tasked with developing a sense of competence and mastery in skills and tasks, or risk feeling inferior and inadequate.

Answer:

QUESTION 128

Rebecca and her husband, David, are having trouble communicating about their finances. Rebecca wants to save money for their children's college education, while David thinks they should focus on paying off their credit card debt first. They have been arguing about this for several months and neither one seems to be able to understand the other's point of view. Which of the following communication skills could help them resolve this conflict?

    A. Ignoring the problem and hoping it will go away

    B. Blaming each other for the problem

    C. Using active listening and paraphrasing to confirm understanding

    D. Trying to convince the other person that they are right

Answer:

QUESTION 129

What is the difference between a fixed expense and a variable expense, and how can understanding this difference help individuals and families manage their finances?

A. A fixed expense is a regular and predictable cost, such as rent or a car payment, while a variable expense is an irregular and unpredictable cost, such as medical bills or car repairs. Understanding the difference between fixed and variable expenses can help individuals and families budget more effectively and plan for unexpected expenses.

B. A fixed expense is an irregular and unpredictable cost, such as medical bills or car repairs, while a variable expense is a regular and predictable cost, such as rent or a car payment. Understanding the difference between fixed and variable expenses can help individuals and families budget more effectively and plan for unexpected expenses.

C. A fixed expense and a variable expense are the same thing, and there is no difference between the two. It is not necessary to distinguish between fixed and variable expenses because they both serve the same purpose.

D. A fixed expense and a variable expense are both subjective terms, and the distinction between the two can vary depending on the individual. It is important to understand each individual's definition of fixed and variable expenses in order to make informed financial decisions.

Answer:

QUESTION 130

How might an individual's early childhood experiences affect their needs, roles, and goals in adulthood?

A. Early childhood experiences have little impact on an individual's needs, roles, and goals in adulthood, which are largely determined by genetics.

B. Early childhood experiences can have a significant impact on an individual's needs, roles, and goals in adulthood, with factors such as attachment style and parental relationships shaping development.

C. Early childhood experiences are only relevant to an individual's needs, roles, and goals if they experienced significant trauma or abuse during this time.

D. Early childhood experiences primarily impact an individual's needs, roles, and goals during adolescence, but become less relevant in adulthood.

Answer:

QUESTION 131

What is the interrelatedness of personal, family, work, and community roles and responsibilities?

A. Each role operates in isolation
B. Personal roles do not affect family, work or community responsibilities
C. Family roles do not affect personal, work or community responsibilities
D. Each role impacts and is impacted by other roles

Answer:

QUESTION 132

What are some potential benefits of family involvement in children's education?

A. Improved academic outcomes, better attendance, and increased motivation
B. Increased likelihood of behavioral problems, decreased school engagement, and poorer performance
C. Reduced interest in learning, decreased social skills, and increased absenteeism
D. No significant impact on academic achievement or school-related outcomes

Answer:

QUESTION 133

Which of the following statements best describes the relationship between socioeconomic status and family well-being?

    A. Families with higher socioeconomic status have better well-being than those with lower socioeconomic status.
    B. Family well-being is not affected by socioeconomic status.
    C. Families with lower socioeconomic status have better well-being than those with higher socioeconomic status.
    D. The relationship between socioeconomic status and family well-being is complex and varies depending on factors such as access to resources and social support.

Answer:

QUESTION 134

Sarah is looking to open a savings account but is unsure which institution to choose. She values personalized customer service and wants to avoid high fees. Which institution is the best option for her?

    A. Credit union
    B. Bank
    C. Insurance company
    D. Payday loan center

Answer:

QUESTION 135

This question is intentionally removed.

QUESTION 136

John is a single father who recently lost his job. He is worried about how he will support his family and meet their needs. What are some community resources that John can access to help him and his family during this difficult time?

    A. Unemployment benefits, food banks, financial assistance programs, and job training programs.
    B. Moving to a new city where he can find better job opportunities.
    C. Selling his assets to make ends meet.
    D. Borrowing money from his friends and family.

Answer:

QUESTION 137

What characteristic of materials is important to consider when selecting furnishings for a home?

    A. Weight
    B. Texture
    C. Scent
    D. Taste

Answer:

QUESTION 138

What is the difference between a debit card and a credit card?

    A. Debit cards are linked to a checking account, while credit cards are not
    B. Debit cards allow individuals to spend money they do not have, while credit cards do not
    C. Debit cards require a PIN number, while credit cards do not
    D. Debit cards do not charge interest, while credit cards do

Answer:

QUESTION 139

Mark has been offered a credit card with a high credit limit and a low interest rate. He is considering using the credit card to purchase a new car. Which of the following is a potential consequence of using a credit card to purchase a car?

    A. Mark will be able to take advantage of low interest rates and flexible repayment options
    B. Mark will have a high credit utilization ratio, which could harm his credit score
    C. Mark will be able to pay off the car more quickly than with a traditional car loan
    D. Mark will have to pay a lower interest rate than he would with a traditional car loan

Answer:

QUESTION 140

Lisa is in the market for a new car and has narrowed her choices down to two models: a gas-powered SUV and a hybrid sedan. Lisa wants to make a wise consumer decision that not only fits her budget but also aligns with her values of reducing carbon footprint. She decides to create a decision matrix to evaluate the two cars based on factors such as price, fuel efficiency, carbon emissions, and safety ratings. Which of the following best describes Lisa's decision-making strategy?

    A. Spontaneous
    B. Rational
    C. Impulsive
    D. Emotional

Answer:

QUESTION 141

You have been given the opportunity to invest in a stock, but you are unsure if it is a good investment. Which of the following factors should you consider before investing in the stock?

    A. The current price of the stock
    B. The company's financial statements and performance
    C. The company's industry and competitors
    D. All of the above

Answer:

QUESTION 142

Maria and her family are struggling to pay their bills due to a sudden reduction in income. What strategy could they use to adjust their resources to meet their financial needs?

    A. Continue spending as usual and hope for a solution to present itself
    B. Seek additional sources of income through a part-time job or side hustle
    C. Ignore the problem and hope it will resolve itself over time
    D. Borrow money from family and friends to cover expenses

Answer:

QUESTION 143

Sarah is a recent college graduate who has just landed her first job. She wants to create a short-term financial management plan to help her manage her finances effectively. Which of the following actions should she take as part of her plan?

    A. Investing a portion of her paycheck in the stock market
    B. Paying off her student loans over the next 10 years
    C. Saving money for a down payment on a house
    D. Planning for her retirement

Answer:

QUESTION 144

John and his wife are planning for retirement and want to ensure they have enough resources to meet their needs. What strategy could they use to select resources to meet their goals?

A. Investing in high-risk stocks without considering their financial situation
B. Consulting with a financial advisor to create a retirement plan
C. Ignoring the issue and hoping they will have enough money when the time comes
D. Putting all of their savings into a single account without diversifying

Answer:

QUESTION 145

Javier signed a contract with a gym for a one-year membership, but after a few months, he no longer wished to continue the membership. When he contacted the gym to cancel, he was informed that he could not cancel until the end of the year and would have to continue paying the monthly fee. What should Javier do to protect his consumer rights?

A. Contact the state attorney general's office to file a complaint.
B. Accept the gym's terms and continue paying the monthly fee.
C. Consult with an attorney to explore legal options.
D. Take no action, as he signed a contract and is obligated to fulfill its terms.

Answer:

QUESTION 146

Mary and John are purchasing a new home and want to ensure that it meets safety standards. What should they look for in the home to ensure that it meets safety standards?

A. Fire extinguishers, smoke alarms, and carbon monoxide detectors
B. Adequate ventilation and insulation
C. Well-maintained electrical wiring and plumbing
D. All of the above

Answer:

QUESTION 147

Which of the following is NOT a factor that affects the quality of apparel construction?

A. The type of fabric used
B. The skill level of the seamstress
C. The color of the thread used
D. The type of stitch used

Answer:

QUESTION 148

Which of the following factors can affect the durability of apparel construction?

A. The type of fabric used
B. The color of the thread used
C. The style of the garment
D. The time of day the garment was constructed

Answer:

QUESTION 149

Which of the following is a key factor that affects money management and financial planning throughout the life cycle?

    A. Education level
    B. Marital status
    C. Physical health
    D. Religious affiliation

Answer:

QUESTION 150

What is a credit score?

    A. The total amount of money a person owes on their credit cards
    B. A numerical rating that represents a person's creditworthiness
    C. The interest rate charged on a loan
    D. The maximum amount a person can borrow on a credit card

Answer:

QUESTION 151

Sarah and her husband want to retire comfortably and are selecting resources to meet their goals. What strategy could they use to select resources?

    A. Putting all of their savings in a single investment account without diversifying
    B. Ignoring the issue and hoping they will have enough money when the time comes
    C. Consulting with a financial advisor to create a retirement plan and diversify their investments
    D. Investing all of their savings in high-risk stocks to potentially earn more money

Answer:

QUESTION 152

Which method can be used to research and compare goods and services when making a consumer decision?

    A. Asking friends and family for their opinions
    B. Making a purchase without researching other options
    C. Reading online reviews and ratings
    D. Only considering the price of the product

Answer:

QUESTION 153

What is a strategy for managing personal and work commitments?

    A. Working overtime to get more done.
    B. Prioritizing tasks based on their level of importance.
    C. Avoiding breaks and working straight through the day.
    D. Taking on additional responsibilities to show dedication.

Answer:

QUESTION 154

What is the difference between a food allergy and a food intolerance?

    A. A food allergy is a reaction of the immune system to a specific food, while a food intolerance is a digestive problem caused by the body's inability to digest a particular food; both involve the body's response to a specific food
    B. A food allergy is a digestive problem caused by the body's inability to digest a particular food, while a food intolerance is a reaction of the immune system to a specific food; both involve the body's response to a specific food
    C. A food allergy and a food intolerance are the same thing and are caused by the body's inability to digest a particular food
    D. A food allergy and a food intolerance are the same thing and are caused by the body's immune response to a specific food

Answer:

QUESTION 155

John and Sarah are a retired couple who have recently moved into a new condo. They are looking to create a comfortable and inviting living room space that accommodates their needs as they age. What design element should they consider to promote safety and ease of movement in the space?

    A. Texture
    B. Color
    C. Lighting
    D. Pattern

Answer:

QUESTION 156

What is the difference between "sell-by" and "use-by" dates on food packaging?

    A. "Sell-by" dates indicate the last day the store should sell the product, while "use-by" dates indicate the last day the product is safe to eat
    B. "Sell-by" dates indicate the last day the product is safe to eat, while "use-by" dates indicate the last day the store should sell the product
    C. "Sell-by" dates indicate the date the product was manufactured, while "use-by" dates indicate the date the product was packaged
    D. "Sell-by" dates indicate the date the product was delivered to the store, while "use-by" dates indicate the date the product was harvested or produced

Answer:

QUESTION 157

When planning a meal, which of the following should be considered?

    A. Nutritional balance and variety
    B. Cost-effectiveness
    C. Ease of preparation
    D. All of the above

Answer:

QUESTION 158

What is the purpose of portion control in meal planning?

    A. To ensure consistent serving sizes
    B. To limit calorie intake
    C. To prevent food waste
    D. To improve food safety

Answer:

QUESTION 159

John is a busy executive who travels frequently for work and also coaches his son's soccer team. He is struggling to find time to manage all of his commitments, and is feeling stressed and overwhelmed. What is a potential resource that John can use to manage his time more effectively?

  A. Hiring a personal assistant to handle tasks.
  B. Cutting back on his work travel.
  C. Having his son quit the soccer team.
  D. Ignoring personal commitments to focus on work.

Answer:

QUESTION 160

Sarah received a letter in the mail informing her that she won a lottery worth $100,000 and needs to pay a small processing fee to claim the prize. The letter included a check for the processing fee, which Sarah deposited into her bank account. A few days later, she received a call from the lottery company asking for additional fees to claim the prize. What should Sarah do?

  A. Pay the additional fees to claim the prize
  B. Contact the lottery company and ask for more information about the fees
  C. Contact her bank and report the check as fraudulent
  D. File a complaint with the Better Business Bureau (BBB)

Answer:

QUESTION 161

Which of the following is a characteristic of iron deficiency?

  A. Fatigue and weakness
  B. Constipation and abdominal pain
  C. Excessive bleeding and bruising
  D. Numbness and tingling in the extremities

Answer:

QUESTION 162

How can meal planning and preparation promote healthy eating habits?

  A. It can reduce the time and effort required to make healthy meals
  B. It can help with portion control and calorie management
  C. It can increase variety and nutrient intake
  D. All of the above

Answer:

QUESTION 163

Which of the following is the best material for cutting boards?

  A. Glass
  B. Marble
  C. Plastic
  D. Wood

Answer:

QUESTION 164

How does cooking affect the nutrient content of foods?

    A. Cooking can cause the loss of certain nutrients, such as vitamin C and B vitamins
    B. Cooking can increase the nutrient content of foods by breaking down certain compounds
    C. Cooking has no effect on the nutrient content of foods
    D. Cooking can only affect the nutrient content of raw foods, not processed foods

Answer:

QUESTION 165

You are a home cook and have invited your friends over for dinner. You are preparing chicken for the main course and have just finished cutting it into pieces. You notice that there are some raw chicken juices on the cutting board. What should you do?

    A. Wipe the cutting board with a paper towel and proceed with cooking
    B. Rinse the cutting board with water and soap before proceeding with cooking
    C. Discard the cutting board and use a new one for cooking
    D. Use the cutting board as is and cook the chicken without cleaning it.

Answer:

QUESTION 166

Which of the following is an effective technique for establishing healthy eating habits in families?

    A. Strictly limiting all processed foods and snacks
    B. Encouraging children to clean their plates
    C. Involving children in meal planning and preparation
    D. Banning all sweets and desserts

Answer:

QUESTION 167

Which of the following is the healthiest type of oil to use for cooking?

    A. Vegetable oil
    B. Coconut oil
    C. Olive oil
    D. Canola oil

Answer:

QUESTION 168

Which of the following is an example of a foodborne illness?

    A. Cuts and lacerations from a knife
    B. Food poisoning from consuming undercooked chicken
    C. Burns from touching a hot stove
    D. Allergic reaction to a food ingredient

Answer:

QUESTION 169

Which agency is responsible for regulating and inspecting meat, poultry, and egg products?

    A. Food and Drug Administration (FDA)
    B. Environmental Protection Agency (EPA)
    C. United States Department of Agriculture (USDA)
    D. Centers for Disease Control and Prevention (CDC)

Answer:

QUESTION 170

Which federal agency is responsible for regulating and inspecting seafood products?

    A. Food and Drug Administration (FDA)
    B. United States Department of Agriculture (USDA)
    C. Environmental Protection Agency (EPA)
    D. National Oceanic and Atmospheric Administration (NOAA)

Answer:

QUESTION 171

Which agency is responsible for enforcing food safety regulations in restaurants and grocery stores?

    A. United States Department of Agriculture (USDA)
    B. Environmental Protection Agency (EPA)
    C. Centers for Disease Control and Prevention (CDC)
    D. Local health department

Answer:

QUESTION 172

Which federal agency is responsible for regulating and inspecting bottled water?

    A. Food and Drug Administration (FDA)
    B. Environmental Protection Agency (EPA)
    C. United States Department of Agriculture (USDA)
    D. Occupational Safety and Health Administration (OSHA)

Answer:

QUESTION 173

Which agency is responsible for investigating foodborne illness outbreaks and coordinating with state and local health departments?

    A. Food and Drug Administration (FDA)
    B. United States Department of Agriculture (USDA)
    C. Centers for Disease Control and Prevention (CDC)
    D. Environmental Protection Agency (EPA)

Answer:

QUESTION 174

Which of the following is the best way to store fresh fruits and vegetables?

    A. In an airtight container
    B. In a paper bag
    C. In a plastic bag with holes punched in it
    D. In a sunny spot on the counter

Answer:

QUESTION 175

When following a recipe, what is the purpose of preheating the oven?

    A. To reduce the cooking time
    B. To ensure even cooking
    C. To prevent the food from sticking to the pan
    D. To make the food taste better

Answer:

QUESTION 176

Sarah is preparing to bake a cake for her friend's birthday, but the recipe calls for 2 cups of sugar, which she thinks is too much. She decides to cut the sugar down to 1 cup, but the cake turns out dry and crumbly. What skill did Sarah fail to apply in this situation?

    A. Interpreting recipes
    B. Converting recipes
    C. Scaling recipes
    D. Modifying recipes

Answer:

QUESTION 177

As a family and consumer sciences teacher, Sarah is responsible for teaching a variety of subjects, including culinary arts, fashion design, and interior design. Which of the following skills is most important for Sarah to have in order to effectively teach these diverse subjects?

    A. Strong public speaking skills
    B. Proficiency in a foreign language
    C. Knowledge of educational theory
    D. Creativity and innovation

Answer:

QUESTION 178

Katie is interested in pursuing a career in nutrition and dietetics. She is considering two job offers: one at a hospital and one at a school. Which of the following work experiences would be most beneficial for Katie to gain the necessary skills and knowledge for a career in nutrition and dietetics?

    A. Working as a cashier in a grocery store
    B. Volunteering at a community center
    C. Interning at a local hospital
    D. Working in retail sales at a clothing store

Answer:

QUESTION 179

Which of the following professions is an entrepreneurial opportunity in the field of family and consumer sciences?

A. Event Planner
B. Electrician
C. Financial Analyst
D. Web Developer

Answer:

QUESTION 180

Which of the following professions falls under the category of clothing and textiles in family and consumer sciences?

A. Social Worker
B. Fashion Designer
C. Veterinarian
D. Real Estate Agent

Answer:

QUESTION 181

You are an employee in a family and consumer science organization and have recently discovered that a colleague is engaged in unethical behavior, such as stealing office supplies and taking credit for work that they did not complete. What should you do in this situation?

A. Ignore the behavior as it is not your responsibility to police your colleagues.
B. Confront the colleague in a public setting to shame them into stopping their behavior.
C. Report the behavior to your supervisor or human resources department.
D. Engage in the same behavior to level the playing field.

Answer:

QUESTION 182

As an employer in a family and consumer science organization, you have received a complaint from an employee about sexual harassment from another employee. What is the appropriate action for you to take?

A. Dismiss the complaint as unfounded and take no action.
B. Investigate the complaint and take appropriate action, such as disciplinary action or termination, if the complaint is substantiated.
C. Ignore the complaint and hope that it goes away on its own.
D. Encourage the employee to ignore the behavior and focus on their work.

Answer:

QUESTION 183

This question is intentionally removed.

QUESTION 184

Which of the following factors should be considered when evaluating career options in Family and Consumer Sciences?

A. Personal interests and strengths
B. Availability of job openings in the chosen field
C. Potential for career growth and advancement
D. Income potential and job security

Answer:

QUESTION 185

Which of the following is the most important factor in building strong customer/client relationships in a family and consumer sciences program?

A. Offering the lowest prices on services and products
B. Providing excellent customer service
C. Providing a wide variety of services and products
D. Offering discounts and promotions to customers/clients

Answer:

QUESTION 186

Which of the following is an example of a customer/client service skill?

A. Communicating effectively
B. Cooking gourmet meals
C. Sewing intricate designs
D. Conducting scientific experiments

Answer:

QUESTION 187

Which of the following is a necessary training requirement for a career in family and consumer sciences?

A. Master's degree in education
B. Certification in a specific area of family and consumer sciences
C. Experience in the hospitality industry
D. Aptitude for science and technology

Answer:

QUESTION 188

Which of the following degrees is typically required for teaching family and consumer sciences in a high school setting?

A. Bachelor's degree in any field
B. Associate's degree in family and consumer sciences
C. Master's degree in education with a specialization in family and consumer sciences
D. Doctoral degree in family and consumer sciences

Answer:

QUESTION 189

In which of the following meal service styles are dishes placed on large platters and passed around the table for guests to serve themselves?

A. Plated service
B. Buffet service
C. Family-style service
D. Cafeteria-style service

Answer:

QUESTION 190

Which of the following is a table setting that is commonly used in formal dining events?

- A. Casual setting
- B. Buffet setting
- C. Formal setting
- D. Picnic setting

Answer:

QUESTION 191

Which of the following personal qualities is important for success in a customer service role?

- A. Lack of patience and understanding
- B. Effective communication skills
- C. Inability to handle stress and pressure
- D. Lack of empathy and compassion

Answer:

QUESTION 192

What is the primary focus of a dietitian?

- A. Developing healthy meal plans for clients
- B. Designing fashion accessories
- C. Conducting legal research for cases
- D. Building furniture

Answer:

QUESTION 193

What is the primary focus of a child and family social worker?

- A. Supporting families in crisis situations
- B. Conducting scientific research on new medications
- C. Managing large-scale construction projects
- D. Performing complex mathematical equations

Answer:

QUESTION 194

What is the primary responsibility of a financial planner?

- A. Helping clients plan for and meet their financial goals
- B. Providing legal advice and representation
- C. Developing and implementing marketing strategies for businesses
- D. Performing complex medical procedures

Answer:

QUESTION 195

How does FCCLA promote civic engagement among students?

    A. By providing opportunities for community service projects
    B. By organizing social events for students
    C. By offering opportunities for students to earn money
    D. By offering career counseling services to students

Answer:

QUESTION 196

How can participation in FCCLA benefit students in their future careers?

    A. By providing networking opportunities with professionals in their field of interest
    B. By teaching students specific job skills
    C. By providing opportunities for internships and job shadowing
    D. All of the above

Answer:

QUESTION 197

Under what circumstances can an employee be exempt from the minimum wage and overtime pay requirements under the Fair Labor Standards Act (FLSA)?

    A. If the employee is a manager or executive.
    B. If the employee is paid on a salary basis and meets certain job duty tests.
    C. If the employer is a nonprofit organization.
    D. If the employee works fewer than 40 hours per week.

Answer:

QUESTION 198

What are the requirements under the Family and Medical Leave Act (FMLA) for covered employers and eligible employees?

    A. Covered employers must provide up to 12 weeks of unpaid leave to eligible employees for any reason.
    B. Covered employers must provide up to 12 weeks of unpaid leave to eligible employees for a serious health condition, the birth or adoption of a child, or to care for a family member with a serious health condition.
    C. Eligible employees must be employed for at least one year to qualify for FMLA leave.
    D. Covered employers are not required to provide job protection for employees on FMLA leave.

Answer:

QUESTION 199

What is the purpose of a cover letter when applying for a job?

    A. To provide a summary of your work history and qualifications.
    B. To express interest in the job and highlight how your skills and experience match the job requirements.
    C. To request an interview and provide a list of references.
    D. To negotiate salary and benefits.

Answer:

QUESTION 200

Which of the following is a common asked during a job interview?

A.   What is your favorite color?
B.   What are your salary expectations?
C.   How would you handle a difficult situation at work?
D.   Have you ever been arrested?

Answer:

QUESTION 201

Which of the following personal qualities is important for success in the workplace?

A.   Lack of self-awareness
B.   Open-mindedness
C.   Inflexibility
D.   Arrogance

Answer:

QUESTION 202

Which of the following personal qualities is important for success in a team environment?

A.   Lack of empathy and understanding
B.   Collaboration and cooperation
C.   Closed-mindedness
D.   Ego-centric behavior

Answer:

QUESTION 203

Which of the following skills is important for success in project management?

A.   Poor organizational skills
B.   Lack of time management skills
C.   Effective delegation skills
D.   Poor communication skills

Answer:

QUESTION 204

Which of the following is a career path in family and consumer sciences that is currently in high demand?

A.   Traditional home economics teacher
B.   Textile manufacturing worker
C.   Nutritionist or dietitian
D.   Restaurant server

Answer:

QUESTION 205

A recent graduate with a degree in interior design is struggling to find a job in their field. Which of the following options would be the best for them?

    A.   Expand their job search to other fields such as marketing or graphic design
    B.   Consider taking additional courses to gain expertise in sustainable design practices
    C.   Pursue an alternative career path that aligns with their skills and interests
    D.   Wait for the job market to improve before applying for new opportunities

Answer:

QUESTION 206

A culinary arts graduate is considering starting their own catering business. What would be the most significant advantage of starting a business in the food industry?

    A.   The ability to work flexible hours
    B.   Access to state-of-the-art equipment
    C.   A stable and predictable income
    D.   The potential for high profits and growth opportunities

Answer:

Chapter 2 – Answers and Explanations

QUESTION 1

Answer: B

Explanation: While all of the factors listed can have an impact on physical development throughout the lifespan, research suggests that nutrition has the greatest impact. Proper nutrition is critical for the growth and development of tissues and organs, and can affect everything from bone density to brain development. Genetics play a role in determining physical characteristics, but they do not have as much influence on physical development as nutrition does. Exercise is important for maintaining physical health, but it does not have as much impact on physical development as nutrition. Environmental factors, such as exposure to toxins or pollutants, can have negative effects on physical development, but they are typically not as significant as the effects of poor nutrition.

QUESTION 2

This question is intentionally removed.

QUESTION 3

Answer: A

Explanation: The addition of a child to the family system can be a major adjustment, and parents/guardians can prepare by establishing a strong support network. This may include seeking the support of family members, friends, and other parents, as well as joining parenting groups or classes. Buying expensive baby gear may be nice to have, but it is not essential for preparing for the addition of a child. Ignoring the changes and continuing with the current lifestyle can be detrimental to the child's well-being and development, and avoiding seeking professional help can limit resources and support.

QUESTION 4

Answer: C

Explanation: Kubler-Ross's stages of grief (denial, anger, bargaining, depression, and acceptance) describe the emotional process that people go through when faced with a terminal illness or other significant loss.

QUESTION 5

Answer: D

Explanation: While it's important to start teaching children about their bodies and appropriate boundaries in early childhood, parents should wait until their child expresses interest or asks questions before discussing more specific topics related to sexuality and relationships. By waiting until the child is ready and interested, parents can ensure that the information they provide is relevant and meaningful to the child.

QUESTION 6

Answer: C

Explanation: A blended family is a family structure that includes children from a previous marriage or relationship, as well as the children of the current marriage or relationship. A family consisting of a married couple and their children is an example of a nuclear family. A family consisting of a single parent and their child is an example of a single-parent family. A family consisting of grandparents raising their grandchildren is an example of a grandparent-headed household.

QUESTION 7

Answer: B

Explanation: The second trimester is often considered the most critical period of fetal development. During this time, the fetus undergoes significant physical and neurological development, including the formation of major organs and the development of the nervous system.

QUESTION 8

Answer: B

Explanation: Emotional development is influenced by a variety of factors, including genetics, environmental factors, and life experiences. However, research suggests that socioeconomic status is one of the most significant factors in emotional development, as it can affect a person's exposure to stress, access to resources and support, and opportunities for positive experiences and relationships.

QUESTION 9

This question is intentionally removed.

QUESTION 10

Answer: A

Explanation: Family mealtime is an important opportunity for families to connect and strengthen their relationships. Research has shown that regular family meals have numerous benefits for both children and adults, including improved nutrition, better communication, and enhanced family relationships. Families can make mealtime more enjoyable and successful by involving children in meal planning and preparation, setting a positive and relaxed atmosphere, and limiting distractions such as technology.

QUESTION 11

Answer: D

Explanation: Maslow's hierarchy of needs suggests that individuals must first satisfy basic physiological needs such as food, water, and shelter before they can move on to higher-level needs such as safety, love and belonging, esteem, and self-actualization.

QUESTION 12

Answer: B

Explanation: Providing emotional support is a responsibility of family members. Other responsibilities may include providing financial support, providing care for children and elderly family members, and contributing to household chores and maintenance. Providing healthcare services and job opportunities are not typically considered responsibilities of family members.

QUESTION 13

Answer: C

Explanation: Children's emotional development is strongly influenced by their relationships with caregivers, and spending quality time with parents can be a powerful way to support emotional well-being. Setting aside regular one-on-one time with her parents would be the most effective strategy for supporting Sarah's emotional development, as it would provide her with a safe and supportive environment to talk about her feelings and concerns, build trust and connection with her parents, and receive emotional support and guidance. While academic tutoring and sports teams can be beneficial for some children, they may not be the best first step for addressing emotional struggles. Telling Sarah to focus on getting better grades may add to her stress and anxiety, rather than alleviating it.

QUESTION 14

Answer: A

Explanation: To effectively manage crises and minimize their impact, individuals can use several strategies. First, it is important to prepare in advance by creating a crisis management plan and practicing emergency response procedures. Communication is also crucial, and individuals should communicate clearly and frequently with those affected by the crisis, providing accurate information and updates. Prioritizing the safety and well-being of individuals and communities, and providing support to those who are affected, is also important. Finally, addressing the root causes of the crisis and working to prevent similar crises from occurring in the future can help to ensure long-term resilience and recovery.

QUESTION 15

Answer: C

Explanation: Providing opportunities for cooperative play and group activities helps children develop social skills such as communication, sharing, and empathy. It also helps them build positive relationships with their peers and develop a sense of community. Forcing children to share or criticizing them for social mistakes can be counterproductive and may even lead to social anxiety or aggression.

QUESTION 16

Answer: D

Explanation: Parenting can be challenging and demanding. Common challenges include finding a balance between work and family responsibilities, managing their own emotional reactions to their children's behavior, and communicating effectively with their children.

QUESTION 17

Answer: C

Explanation: Access to safe and supportive environments is crucial for fostering optimal physical, emotional, social, and cognitive development. This includes access to safe and secure housing, positive social networks, and supportive relationships with caregivers, teachers, and mentors.

QUESTION 18

Answer: A

Explanation: Families with children with special needs may face various challenges in accessing appropriate services and support, such as lack of resources, limited access to specialized professionals, and discrimination or bias. Special education advocacy groups and legal resources can provide families with information and support to navigate the complex systems and laws related to special education services. General education curriculum and mainstreaming programs may be helpful for some students with special needs, but they do not address the individualized needs of students with significant disabilities. Private tutoring and specialized therapy services may be helpful for some families, but they may not be accessible or affordable for all families. Community support groups and disability organizations can provide emotional support and connections to other families with similar experiences, but they may not provide the specific information and resources needed to navigate the special education system.

QUESTION 19

Answer: C

Explanation: Healthy interpersonal relationships are characterized by mutual respect and trust, open and honest communication, empathy and understanding, and a willingness to work through challenges together. A lack of communication, a focus on power dynamics, and a lack of empathy are all characteristics of unhealthy interpersonal relationships that can be detrimental to well-being.

QUESTION 20

Answer: C

Explanation: Ignoring the situation or encouraging the student to handle it on their own is not helpful and may worsen the situation. Punishing the student for poor academic performance may not address the root cause of the issue. Offering support and resources to help the student address their personal issues can show that you care about their well-being and may help improve their academic performance.

QUESTION 21

Answer: B

Explanation: Engaging in physical activities is crucial for promoting physical development, and can also have a positive impact on cognitive and social development. By encouraging the child to participate in sports or dance, the parent is promoting multiple areas of development.

QUESTION 22

Answer: C

Explanation: Community playgroups and parent-child classes can provide infants and young children with opportunities for social interaction and play, which are critical for their cognitive and social development. Social media groups, children's television programs, video games, and smartphone apps are not recommended resources for promoting optimal development in infants and young children.

QUESTION 23

Answer: B

Explanation: In a situation where a student is having a severe allergic reaction, it is important to act quickly. The first thing to do is to administer the student's epinephrine auto-injector if they have one, as this can help to stop the reaction from worsening. Calling 911 should be done after administering the auto-injector if the symptoms persist or worsen.

QUESTION 24

Answer: B

Explanation: Interpersonal relationships are important for supporting well-being in a number of ways, including providing emotional support, social connection, and a sense of belonging. In addition, research has shown that strong interpersonal relationships can have a positive impact on physical health outcomes, including lower rates of chronic disease, reduced risk of cardiovascular disease, and better immune function. Increased stress and anxiety, decreased social support, and a decreased sense of belonging are all potential negative outcomes associated with poor interpersonal relationships.

QUESTION 25

Answer: B

Explanation: Providing extra support and resources can help the student overcome their learning disability and improve their academic skills. This is an effective strategy for promoting academic development and ensuring that the student has the tools they need to succeed.

QUESTION 26

Answer: A

Explanation: Single parents often face a variety of challenges, including financial instability, social isolation, and limited access to childcare. Family and friends who can provide emotional support and assistance with childcare can be invaluable resources in helping single parents to overcome these challenges. While government-sponsored programs, community-based organizations, and faith-based organizations can also be helpful, they may not always be accessible or appropriate for every single parent.

QUESTION 27

Answer: B

Explanation: Conflict and crisis are inevitable in any family, but the way in which they are managed can make all the difference. Healthy conflict resolution strategies include active listening, expressing oneself clearly and respectfully, seeking compromise, and working towards a solution that benefits all members of the family. Avoiding conflict or blaming others for the problem will only lead to further conflict and dysfunction within the family.

QUESTION 28

Answer: B

Explanation: Piaget's sensorimotor stage (birth to 2 years) is characterized by the development of object permanence, which is the understanding that objects continue to exist even when they are not directly perceived.

QUESTION 29

Answer: C

Explanation: Non-normative life events are events that are not common to most people in a particular culture or society, such as experiencing a natural disaster, losing a limb, or being diagnosed with a serious illness. Graduating from college, getting married, and retiring from work are normative life events.

QUESTION 30

Answer: C

Explanation: Authoritative parenting style involves warmth, affection, clear rules and consequences, and open communication. Parents who adopt this style have high expectations for behavior, but also provide support and guidance to their children.

QUESTION 31

Answer: C

Explanation: Using "I" statements instead of "you" statements can help individuals communicate their own perspectives and needs without coming across as accusatory or judgmental. This approach can promote understanding and empathy in relationships.

QUESTION 32

Answer: B

Explanation: Community involvement can provide individuals with a sense of purpose and fulfillment, which can have a positive impact on their personal and family roles and responsibilities. By engaging in activities that are meaningful to them and contribute to the community, individuals may feel a greater sense of satisfaction and purpose in their lives, which can in turn lead to improved relationships and a greater sense of well-being. However, it's important to balance community involvement with personal and family responsibilities to avoid neglecting those important roles.

QUESTION 33

Answer: B

Explanation: Nonverbal communication cues refer to the use of body language, facial expressions, and gestures to convey meaning. Nodding is an example of a nonverbal cue that typically signifies agreement or understanding.

QUESTION 34

This question is intentionally removed.

QUESTION 35

Answer: C

Explanation: The primary goal of parenting is to prepare the child for adulthood by teaching them important life skills and values that will enable them to become responsible and independent adults.

QUESTION 36

Answer: A

Explanation: Piaget's theory states that children progress through these four stages of cognitive development from birth through adulthood, with each stage building upon the previous one.

QUESTION 37

Answer: D

Explanation: Factors that can affect parenting styles, expectations, and responsibilities include cultural background, family values, socio-economic status, education level, and family structure, among others. Hair color is not a relevant factor in this context.

QUESTION 38

Answer: A

Explanation: Poverty can have a wide range of negative consequences on families and children, including limited access to resources, poor health outcomes, and educational challenges. Increased social support, better family cohesion, and enhanced creativity are not necessarily associated with poverty. Improved mental health, increased access to healthcare, and better job opportunities are also not necessarily a consequence of poverty. Stronger family ties, increased opportunities for social mobility, and improved overall well-being may be possible outcomes, but are not guaranteed.

QUESTION 39

Answer: B

Explanation: In a command economy, the government makes all economic decisions and allocates resources. This means that consumers have no influence over the production or allocation of goods and services, as these decisions are made by the government. Consumers may be allocated certain goods and services based on their needs, but they do not have the freedom to choose which goods and services they purchase. Option a) is incorrect because consumers do not have the freedom to purchase any goods or services they want in a command economy. Option c) is incorrect because while consumers may be required to purchase certain goods and services, this is not the primary impact of a command economy on consumer behavior. Option d) is incorrect because

QUESTION 40

Answer: C

Explanation: The most important thing parents can do to keep their child safe is to keep potentially dangerous items out of their reach. This can include chemicals, sharp objects, and other hazardous materials.

QUESTION 41

Answer: C

Explanation: This attachment style is characterized by a child's avoidance of caregivers and lack of interest in forming close relationships with them. The child may appear indifferent or detached from adults, and may not seek comfort from them when upset. The student's difficulty forming attachments to caregivers suggests they may be exhibiting an avoidant attachment style.

QUESTION 42

Answer: A

Explanation: Parenting style can be influenced by a number of factors, but some of the most significant ones include cultural background (e.g. parenting practices that are considered normal in one culture may not be in another), personal values (e.g. some parents may prioritize independence while others may prioritize obedience), and the child's temperament (e.g. an easygoing child may be raised differently than a difficult one).

QUESTION 43

Answer: A

Explanation: Studies have shown that income is the primary factor that affects family well-being. Families with higher incomes generally have better access to resources such as healthcare, education, and healthy food.

QUESTION 44

Answer: D

Explanation: Student loan servicers are businesses that handle student loan repayment for the federal government or private lenders. They offer a variety of loan options, such as federal student loans, private student loans, and parent PLUS loans. Credit card companies and payday loan centers typically do not provide loans for higher education, while mortgage lenders provide loans for purchasing homes.

QUESTION 45

Answer: A

Explanation: Needs are essential for survival and include things like food, water, shelter, and clothing. Wants, on the other hand, are things that are desired but not necessary for survival. It is important to distinguish between the two because prioritizing needs over wants can help individuals and families make wise financial decisions and avoid unnecessary expenses that can lead to financial hardship.

QUESTION 46

Answer: A

Explanation: In Vygotsky's theory, language and communication are seen as critical components of cognitive development, allowing individuals to internalize knowledge and scaffold their own learning. Piaget's theory, in contrast, views language development as a byproduct of cognitive development, rather than a key factor in it.

QUESTION 47

Answer: C

Explanation: While genetics may play a significant role in determining certain traits, such as physical appearance or intelligence, environmental factors such as upbringing, education, and socialization can also have a profound impact on an individual's needs, roles, and goals.

QUESTION 48

Answer: B

Explanation: Neglect is the failure to provide for a child's basic needs, including food, clothing, shelter, medical care, and supervision. Poor hygiene, such as dirty clothes or an unkempt appearance, is one of the signs of neglect. Unexplained bruises and injuries are signs of physical abuse, and sudden changes in behavior may indicate emotional abuse. Option d) "All of the above" is not a valid answer as it includes signs of different types of abuse.

QUESTION 49

Answer: D

Explanation: HUD provides financial assistance to low-income families through various programs, such as the Housing Choice Voucher Program (Section 8) and the HOME Investment Partnerships Program. Jessica can contact her local HUD office or visit the HUD website to learn more about the programs and eligibility requirements. The IRS is responsible for collecting taxes, while the FDIC insures banks and thrift institutions against loss. The SSA administers Social Security, which provides retirement, disability, and survivor benefits, but may not be the best option for Jessica's current situation.

QUESTION 50

Answer: C

Explanation: An external influence refers to factors outside of an individual's personal control that can impact their purchasing decisions. Peer pressure and social norms can be strong external influences that may influence a person to buy certain products or brands in order to fit in with their social group or adhere to societal expectations.

QUESTION 51

Answer: A

Explanation: When selecting furnishings and equipment for a home, it is important to consider their durability. Furnishings and equipment that are built to last will provide a better value in the long run, as they will not need to be replaced as frequently. This can also help to reduce waste and promote sustainability.

QUESTION 52

Answer: A

Explanation: A budget is a financial plan that outlines an individual's or household's expected income and expenses over a certain period of time. It helps individuals manage their money and reach their financial goals.

QUESTION 53

Answer: A

Explanation: When applying for credit, lenders typically look at factors such as a person's employment status and income to determine their creditworthiness. Lenders want to ensure that borrowers have a stable source of income and are able to repay their debts. Age, gender, race, and ethnicity are not factors that should be considered when determining eligibility for credit.

QUESTION 54

Answer: A

Explanation: Secondary sources of information are those that are not directly provided by the manufacturer or seller. A laptop review blog written by a tech enthusiast is an example of a secondary source of information as it is not associated with the manufacturer or seller, and provides an independent opinion about the product.

QUESTION 55

Answer: C

Explanation: When you lease a car, you are essentially renting it for a set period of time. At the end of the lease, you must return the car to the leasing company. This can be a disadvantage if you have become attached to the car or if you have made modifications to it that you will have to remove. Additionally, you do not own the car at the end of the lease, so you will not have an asset to sell or trade in for a new car.

QUESTION 56

Answer: A

Explanation: When selecting furniture for a family room, it is important to consider the size of the furniture relative to the size of the room. Oversized furniture can make the room feel cramped, while undersized furniture can make it feel empty. Style and color are also important considerations, but they should not take precedence over functionality. Durability of the material is also important, as the furniture in a family room is likely to be used frequently. Price is also a consideration, but it should be balanced against the quality and durability of the furniture.

QUESTION 57

Answer: A

Explanation: Savings accounts are designed for individuals to save money over time and earn interest on their balance. Checking accounts, on the other hand, are used for daily transactions and typically do not

QUESTION 58

Answer: C

Explanation: Adjusting a resource means modifying it to fit changing circumstances. Buying a smaller home when your children move out is an example of adjusting a resource to meet changing circumstances.

QUESTION 59

Answer: C

Explanation: Heuristics are mental shortcuts or rules of thumb that help people make quick and efficient decisions. In this case, Maria can use a heuristic by deciding to choose the phone that has the highest overall rating or the phone with the most positive customer reviews, without going into the specifics of the

QUESTION 60

Answer: D

Explanation: With a fixed-rate mortgage, the interest rate is set for the entire duration of the loan. This means that even if interest rates decrease, you will still be paying the same rate. While this can provide stability and predictability in your monthly payments, it can also mean that you are paying a higher interest rate than you would with an adjustable-rate

QUESTION 61

Answer: B

Explanation: Job security is a key factor that can affect an individual's ability to manage their finances in the short-term. An unstable job or sudden job loss can lead to financial difficulties and disrupt an individual's financial plan. Age, homeownership, and political affiliation can also impact financial planning, but they typically have a more long-term effect on an individual's financial stability.

QUESTION 62

Answer: A

Explanation: Selling her car and using public transportation is a strategy for adapting resources to meet needs. Ignoring bills, borrowing money from payday lenders, and continuing to use credit cards can lead to further financial difficulties.

QUESTION 63

Answer: B

Explanation: The FDA is responsible for enforcing laws related to food safety, including ensuring that food is safe, wholesome, and properly labeled.

QUESTION 64

Answer: C

Explanation: Prioritizing your expenses is a step involved in developing a budget. This involves determining which expenses are essential and which can be cut back in order to reach your financial goals.

QUESTION 65

Answer: A

Explanation: Insurance is a means of protecting against financial losses that may arise from unexpected events, such as accidents, illness, or natural disasters.

QUESTION 66

Answer: B

Explanation: Fixed expenses are costs that remain the same each month such as rent, mortgage, and car payments. Variable expenses, on the other hand, are costs that can change from month to month such as groceries, entertainment, and clothing. Knowing the difference between these two types of expenses is important when creating a budget as it allows you to plan for and anticipate changes in your monthly expenses.

QUESTION 67

Answer: A

Explanation: A traditional IRA allows individuals to contribute pre-tax dollars, which can be deducted from their taxable income for that year. This can help to lower their overall tax bill. However, withdrawals during retirement are taxed at the individual's ordinary income tax rate.

QUESTION 68

Answer: D

Explanation: Installing low-flow faucets and showerheads can significantly reduce the amount of water used in the home, as they limit the flow of water while still providing adequate water pressure. Taking shorter showers and watering your lawn less frequently can also help conserve water.

QUESTION 69

Answer: A

Explanation: Polyester is a synthetic fabric known for its durability, strength, and resistance to wrinkles and shrinking. It is commonly used in outdoor clothing and equipment such as jackets, tents, and backpacks.

QUESTION 70

Answer: D

Explanation: Proteins play an important role in food science by providing structure and texture to foods. For example, proteins in meat help give it its texture and chewiness, while proteins in baked goods help provide their structure and ability to rise. Proteins also play a role in browning reactions, but their primary function is to provide structure and texture.

QUESTION 71

Answer: A

Explanation: Celiac disease is an autoimmune disorder in which the body cannot tolerate gluten, a protein found in wheat, barley, and rye. If left untreated, celiac disease can damage the lining of the small intestine and lead to malabsorption of nutrients, including iron. Iron deficiency anemia is a common complication of celiac disease.

QUESTION 72

Answer: B

Explanation: Consumer fraud refers to deceptive or illegal practices used by businesses to take advantage of consumers. Falsely claiming that a product can cure a disease is an example of consumer fraud because it is a false and deceptive claim that preys on people's health concerns.

QUESTION 73

Answer: B

Explanation: Synthetic fibers such as polyester and nylon are popular for use in outdoor apparel because they are moisture-wicking, meaning they can pull sweat away from the body and keep the wearer dry. This is especially important for outdoor activities where the body can sweat a lot and damp clothing can lead to discomfort or even hypothermia in cold weather.

QUESTION 74

Answer: B

Explanation: The four types of heat transfer are conduction, convection, radiation, and induction. Conduction occurs when heat is transferred through direct contact between two objects, such as when a pot of water heats the food inside of it. Convection occurs when heat is transferred through a fluid or gas, such as when heated air circulates around a baking dish. Radiation occurs when heat is transferred through electromagnetic waves, such as when food is heated in a microwave. Induction occurs when heat is transferred through a magnetic field, such as when cooking with an induction stove. When cooking food in a pot of boiling water, the heat transfer that occurs is conduction.

QUESTION 75

Answer: A

Explanation: Temperature is a critical factor in food safety, as it can affect the growth of microorganisms in food. For example, foods that are stored at room temperature for extended periods of time are more susceptible to bacterial growth and spoilage.

QUESTION 76

Answer: B

Explanation: Scammers often use phone calls or emails to obtain personal information from unsuspecting victims. To avoid falling prey to such scams, it's important to verify the authenticity of the request by contacting the institution directly using a trusted phone number or email address.

QUESTION 77

Answer: D

Explanation: Cotton fabric is lightweight and breathable, making it a good choice for warm weather clothing. Cotton fibers are soft and allow air to circulate, which helps keep the wearer cool and comfortable in hot weather. This is why cotton is often used for t-shirts, shorts, and other summer clothing items.

QUESTION 78

Answer: B

Explanation: The FDA has established specific criteria that must be met in order for a food to be labeled as "organic". This label indicates that the food has been produced using methods that promote ecological balance and conserve biodiversity, and that synthetic fertilizers, pesticides, and genetically modified organisms (GMOs) have not been used in the production process. The other labels listed - "natural", "low-fat", and "made with whole grains" - are not regulated by the FDA and do not have specific criteria that must be met in order to use these labels.

QUESTION 79

Answer: A

Explanation: The %DV on a food label indicates the percentage of the recommended daily intake for each nutrient that is provided by one serving of the food. This information can be used to help consumers make informed decisions about their nutrient intake and to compare the nutrient content of different foods. The other options listed are not related to the %DV on a food label.

QUESTION 80

Answer: B

Explanation: Leaving chicken (or any perishable food) at room temperature for more than two hours can allow harmful bacteria to multiply rapidly, which can increase the risk of foodborne illness. Washing the chicken with hot water is not recommended, as this can actually spread bacteria around the kitchen. Freezing the chicken will not kill any bacteria that may be present, and cooking it at a higher temperature may not be effective in eliminating all bacteria. The safest option is to discard the chicken and choose a different protein source for the meal.

QUESTION 81

Answer: B

Explanation: Cost-plus pricing is a pricing strategy where the selling price is determined by adding a markup percentage to the cost of the ingredients and other expenses associated with the dish. This pricing strategy ensures that the cost of the dish is covered while still being competitive. Markup pricing, competition-based pricing, and skimming pricing may not take into account the actual cost of the dish, leading to either underpricing or overpricing.

QUESTION 82

Answer: A

Explanation: Portion control is an effective way to reduce costs while still providing a satisfying meal for guests. By reducing the portion sizes of each dish, Sarah can lower the amount of food required for the meal, which will also lower the cost. Switching to lower quality ingredients or eliminating a course may compromise the quality of the meal and eliminate the pleasure of the dining experience.

QUESTION 83

Answer: C

Explanation: Maria is juggling a lot of responsibilities and feeling overwhelmed, so one potential strategy that can help her manage her personal and family commitments is to set aside dedicated time each week for self-care activities. This can include things like exercise, meditation, or spending time with friends or family. By prioritizing her own well-being, she may find that she has more energy and motivation to tackle her other commitments.

QUESTION 84

Answer: C

Explanation: Folic acid is a special nutritional need for pregnant women, as it is important for the development of the baby's brain and nervous system.

QUESTION 85

Answer: D

Explanation: In case of a kitchen emergency, the appropriate action depends on the nature of the emergency. For example, if there is a fire, you should use a fire extinguisher to put it out. Evacuating the building may also be necessary, depending on the severity of the situation. Calling a friend or using water to put out a grease fire, however, are not recommended actions.

QUESTION 86

Answer: A

Explanation: Keeping raw meat at room temperature for several hours is a common kitchen safety hazard related to food handling. It can lead to the growth of harmful bacteria that can cause foodborne illness. Using a sharp knife, washing fruits and vegetables thoroughly, and storing dry goods in airtight containers are all examples of safe and recommended food handling practices.

QUESTION 87

Answer: B

Explanation: The glycemic index is a measure of how quickly a food raises blood sugar levels. Low-glycemic index foods are those with a score of 55 or less. Brown rice has a score of 50, making it a good option for those looking to manage blood sugar levels. White bread, watermelon, and instant oatmeal all have higher glycemic index scores.

QUESTION 88

Answer: A

Explanation: This is important to remove any bacteria or germs that could potentially contaminate the food.

QUESTION 89

Answer: C

Explanation: Eating a variety of foods is a principle of healthy eating. Consuming a diverse range of foods can provide a balance of essential nutrients such as protein, carbohydrates, fats, vitamins, and minerals. Restricting certain food groups, such as fats or carbohydrates, can lead to nutrient deficiencies and imbalanced diets. Additionally, consuming only organic foods is not necessary for a healthy diet, as conventionally grown fruits and vegetables are also nutritious and safe to eat.

QUESTION 90

Answer: A

Explanation: Income level is a significant factor that can affect food choices, food customs, and eating habits. People with lower incomes may have limited access to healthy food options, which can lead to poor dietary choices. They may also prioritize buying cheap, processed food items over fresh produce or lean meats, due to financial constraints. On the other hand, people with higher incomes may have more access to fresh, healthy food options and may have the means to afford more expensive foods, leading to different food customs and eating habits. Hair color, favorite TV show, and height are not factors that have been shown to have a significant impact on food choices or eating habits.

QUESTION 91

Answer: C

Explanation: Cross-contamination occurs when harmful bacteria from one food item is transferred to another food item. Raw meat and ready-to-eat foods should always be kept separate to prevent this from happening. Using separate cutting boards for different types of food and washing hands frequently are also important, but keeping raw meat and ready-to-eat foods separate is the most effective way to prevent cross-contamination.

QUESTION 92

Answer: C

Explanation: Plated service, also known as formal service, is a meal service style where food is portioned and served on individual plates. It is common in formal events such as weddings and business dinners.

QUESTION 93

Answer: B

Explanation: While a blender can be used for many kitchen tasks, it is not the ideal tool for creaming butter and sugar together. The high speed of the blender blades can overwork the mixture, leading to a dense, heavy cake.

QUESTION 94

Answer: C

Explanation: Food advertising has been shown to influence food choices and dietary habits, particularly among children and adolescents. Advertising for unhealthy, high-calorie foods and beverages can lead to overconsumption of these products and contribute to the obesity epidemic. Conversely, advertising for healthy foods can promote healthier dietary habits. While advertising is not the sole determinant of food choices or dietary habits, it can play a significant role in shaping consumer attitudes and behaviors.

QUESTION 95

Answer: A

Explanation: Genetic modification can be used to enhance the nutrient content of crops by introducing genes that increase the production of certain nutrients, such as vitamin A. This can help to address nutrient deficiencies in certain populations.

QUESTION 96

Answer: D

Explanation: Having regular healthy potlucks and cooking demonstrations is a recommended technique for promoting healthy eating habits in workplaces. This can encourage employees to try new foods and learn about healthy meal preparation techniques, as well as provide opportunities for socializing and team building. Providing only healthy food options in vending machines and break rooms can also be helpful, but mandating that all employees bring their own lunch from home and offering free junk food and soda to employees are not effective techniques and may be counterproductive.

QUESTION 97

Answer: B

Explanation: A bacon cheeseburger, fried chicken with mashed potatoes and gravy, and pepperoni pizza are all high in saturated fat and sodium, which can worsen high blood pressure. Grilled salmon with quinoa and roasted vegetables, on the other hand, is a healthy option as it is high in omega-3 fatty acids, fiber, and vitamins and minerals.

QUESTION 98

Answer: D

Explanation: Attention to detail is crucial for a career in family and consumer sciences, which involves working with food, textiles, and other materials that require precise measurements and handling. This skill helps ensure safety, quality, and accuracy in various tasks, such as recipe development, garment construction, and interior design.

QUESTION 99

Answer: C

Explanation: Nutrition and dietetics involves working with individuals and groups to promote healthy eating habits and manage health conditions through diet. Experience working in a hospital or healthcare setting is highly relevant, as this provides exposure to medical conditions, treatment plans, and dietary restrictions. This experience can be gained through internships, volunteer work, or paid employment.

QUESTION 100

Answer: B

Explanation: Providing additional support and guidance can help alleviate the customer's concerns and build a strong relationship with them. This involves offering personalized assistance, providing clear instructions, and demonstrating patience and empathy. Suggesting that they take a different class, telling them that sewing is easy to learn, or encouraging them to bring a friend or family member may not address their specific concerns and may lead to further hesitation or dissatisfaction.

QUESTION 101

Answer: A

Explanation: Family and consumer sciences professions encompass a wide range of fields, including food and nutrition, clothing and textiles, interior design, and consumer economics. A career as a chef falls under the food and nutrition category, which is a major area of family and consumer sciences. Chefs create and prepare meals that are nutritious, healthy, and appealing to consumers. They also manage kitchen operations, supervise staff, and ensure food safety standards are met. While mechanical engineering, law, and architecture are all important professions, they are not directly related to family and consumer sciences.

QUESTION 102

This question is intentionally removed.

QUESTION 103

Answer: B

Explanation: Honesty and integrity are crucial ethical behaviors that facilitate success in leadership. Leaders who demonstrate honesty and integrity gain the trust and respect of their team members, and are more likely to inspire loyalty and commitment.

QUESTION 104

Answer: D

Explanation: Attending trade shows and networking events is an effective way to connect with other sustainable fashion professionals and learn about the latest trends and practices in the industry. By building relationships with others in the field, the graduate can gain valuable insights and opportunities for collaboration or employment.

QUESTION 105

This question is intentionally removed.

QUESTION 106

Answer: C

Explanation: Employers often look for candidates who exhibit a positive attitude and a strong work ethic. These qualities indicate that the candidate will be reliable, hardworking, and motivated to succeed.

QUESTION 107

Answer: D

Explanation: There are several methods that can be used for exploring career opportunities in Family and Consumer Sciences. These include researching job descriptions and requirements to gain a better understanding of what a specific career entails, conducting informational interviews with professionals in the field to learn about their experiences, and participating in job shadowing or internships to gain hands-on experience. Each of these methods can provide valuable insight into different career paths within the field.

QUESTION 108

Answer: B

Explanation: Family and consumer sciences career paths are evolving with the changing economic landscape, and one of the prominent trends is the increasing demand for professionals with skills in technology and design. With the advent of new technologies and digital platforms, professionals in these fields are required to adapt to new ways of communication, data management, and product development. This trend is evident in various subfields of family and consumer sciences, such as fashion design, interior design, culinary arts, and consumer research. Therefore, option b) is the correct answer. Options a), c), and d) are incorrect as they do not reflect the current trend in employment opportunities in family and consumer sciences.

QUESTION 109

Answer: D

Explanation: While it can be tempting to submit multiple applications to increase your chances of getting hired, this approach can actually backfire by making you appear unfocused and lacking in direction. Instead, it's important to research the company and position, tailor your resume and cover letter to the job posting, and follow up with the employer after submitting your application.

QUESTION 110

Answer: C

Explanation: The Americans with Disabilities Act (ADA) requires public accommodations, such as restaurants, stores, and public buildings, to remove existing barriers to accessibility if it is readily achievable to do so. This means that the removal of barriers must be easily accomplishable and able to be carried out without much difficulty or expense. In addition, new construction projects must comply with accessibility requirements, and state and local government agencies are also required to comply with accessibility requirements.

QUESTION 111

Answer: C

Explanation: As a manager, it is important to address performance issues in a constructive and respectful manner. Scheduling a private meeting with the employee allows you to discuss the issues in a one-on-one setting and avoid embarrassing the employee in front of their colleagues. During the meeting, you should provide specific examples of the employee's behavior and work with them to develop a plan for improvement. Firing the employee immediately or ignoring the issue are not effective solutions and may cause further problems within the team.

QUESTION 112

Answer: B

Explanation: Personal training is a profession that falls under the category of food and nutrition in family and consumer sciences. Personal trainers work with clients to develop customized exercise and nutrition plans to help them achieve their fitness goals.

QUESTION 113

Answer: C

Explanation: Discussing the consequences of debt and strategies for debt management would be the most effective strategy for promoting financial responsibility. This involves educating students on the risks associated with borrowing and the importance of living within their means. Encouraging students to use credit cards for everyday purchases may lead to a cycle of debt and financial instability. Demonstrating how to budget for short-term goals only may not prepare students for long-term financial planning. Promoting impulse buying and immediate gratification can lead to overspending and debt.

QUESTION 114

Answer: A

Explanation: The purpose of FCCLA is to provide students with opportunities to develop leadership, communication, and critical thinking skills. FCCLA helps students learn how to work in teams, make decisions, and solve problems while developing their leadership abilities.

QUESTION 115

Answer: B

Explanation: Transparency is an ethical behavior that involves honesty, openness, and clear communication. In the workplace, transparency can help to build trust, promote collaboration, and prevent misunderstandings or conflicts.

QUESTION 116

Answer: B

Explanation: Regular physical activity and exercise are critical for optimal physical, emotional, social, and cognitive development from early childhood throughout the life span. Exercise can help children develop gross and fine motor skills, improve their concentration and memory, reduce stress and anxiety, and promote social interaction and teamwork. Encouraging children to spend long hours watching TV or playing video games, criticizing and shaming children for their mistakes and failures, and allowing children to consume unhealthy food and sugary drinks can have negative effects on physical, emotional, social, and cognitive development.

QUESTION 117

Answer: A

Explanation: Natural disasters can be devastating for families, often resulting in the loss of their home and possessions. FEMA provides disaster assistance to help families get back on their feet, providing financial assistance for temporary housing, home repairs, and other disaster-related expenses.

QUESTION 118

Answer: A

Explanation: Parents play an important role in promoting the physical health and well-being of their children, and setting a good example by modeling healthy behaviors themselves is one of the most effective ways to encourage their children to adopt healthy habits. Enrolling their children in extracurricular activities that promote physical activity and monitoring their children's diets can also be effective strategies, but they are not as impactful as modeling healthy behaviors. Punishing children for engaging in unhealthy behaviors is not an effective strategy and may have negative consequences for their overall well-being.

QUESTION 119

Answer: B

Explanation: Effective communication is a critical skill for building and maintaining healthy family relationships. This includes active listening, expressing oneself clearly and respectfully, and being open to feedback and compromise.

QUESTION 120

Answer: A

Explanation: It's important to properly clean and store bottles and breastmilk to prevent contamination and ensure the baby's health. According to the Centers for Disease Control and Prevention (CDC), bottles should be washed after every use with soap and hot water and then sterilized once a day. Breastmilk can be stored in the refrigerator for up to 72 hours, but should not be refrozen once thawed.

QUESTION 121

Answer: C

Explanation: Ignoring the situation or asking parents to handle it may not be effective in addressing the conflict. Suspending students may worsen the situation and not provide an opportunity for them to learn conflict resolution skills. Facilitating a discussion among the students can help them understand each other's perspectives, address the root cause of the conflict, and find a solution together.

QUESTION 122

Answer: A

Explanation: Becoming a parent/guardian is a major life decision that requires careful consideration of various factors. One such factor is financial stability and resources, as having a child can be expensive and require significant financial investment. While gender identity may also be a consideration for some individuals, it is not directly related to the financial responsibility of raising a child. Height and weight and favorite color are irrelevant to the decision of becoming a parent/guardian.

QUESTION 123

Answer: D

Explanation: Providing tutoring or academic support services, encouraging extracurricular activities, and setting high expectations for academic performance are all ways that parents can support their child's academic success. By providing academic support, parents help their children overcome obstacles and improve their skills. Encouraging extracurricular activities can help children develop a range of skills and interests that can enhance their academic performance. Setting high expectations for academic performance can motivate children to work hard and achieve their goals.

QUESTION 124

Answer: D

Explanation: Parents have a key responsibility in their children's education, which includes ensuring that their children attend school regularly, helping with homework and projects, and encouraging their children to pursue extracurricular activities.

QUESTION 125

Answer: A

Explanation: Interrupting the speaker can prevent them from fully expressing their thoughts and feelings, which can lead to misunderstandings and frustration. It can also signal to the speaker that their ideas are not valued or respected, which can damage the relationship.

QUESTION 126

Answer: D

Explanation: Consumer behavior has a significant impact on the U.S. economy. When consumers are confident and spending money, this can lead to economic growth by increasing demand for goods and services, which in turn drives production and employment. On the other hand, when consumers are hesitant to spend money, this can lead to a decrease in demand for goods and services, which can lead to economic recession. Therefore, understanding consumer behavior is crucial for businesses and policymakers alike in order to promote economic growth and stability. Option a) is incorrect because consumer behavior does have an impact on the U.S. economy. Option b) is correct, but incomplete; consumer behavior influences demand, which in turn drives production and employment. Option c) is incorrect because consumer behavior impacts both local and national economies.

QUESTION 127

Answer: A

Explanation: During adolescence, individuals are trying to establish their own identity and may experiment with different roles and values. Successful resolution of this stage leads to a sense of self and the ability to stay true to oneself, while a lack of resolution can result in confusion and lack of direction.

QUESTION 128

Answer: C

Explanation: Active listening involves paying close attention to what the other person is saying, and then summarizing or paraphrasing their message to confirm that you understand it correctly. This can help build empathy and understanding between Rebecca and David, and make it easier for them to find a compromise that meets both of their needs. Ignoring the problem or blaming each other will only make the conflict worse, while trying to convince the other person that they are right is unlikely to be effective if both parties are deeply entrenched in their positions.

QUESTION 129

Answer: A

Explanation: Fixed expenses are regular and predictable costs that remain the same each month, such as rent or a car payment. Variable expenses, on the other hand, are irregular and unpredictable costs that can vary from month to month, such as medical bills or car repairs. Understanding the difference between fixed and variable expenses can help individuals and families budget more effectively and plan for unexpected expenses by setting aside money for variable expenses and making sure fixed expenses are covered first.

QUESTION 130

Answer: B

Explanation: Early childhood experiences can shape an individual's beliefs and attitudes, as well as their ability to form and maintain relationships. Factors such as parental support and childhood trauma can have lasting effects on an individual's needs, roles, and goals throughout the life span.

QUESTION 131

Answer: D

Explanation: Personal, family, work, and community roles and responsibilities are all interconnected and affect each other. A person's personal responsibilities, such as taking care of their health, can impact their ability to fulfill their work responsibilities. A person's work responsibilities can impact their ability to fulfill their family responsibilities. Additionally, community involvement can impact all aspects of a person's life, including their personal, family, and work responsibilities. It's important to recognize the interrelatedness of these roles and responsibilities in order to effectively manage them and maintain a healthy work-life balance.

QUESTION 132

Answer: A

Explanation: Research has consistently shown that family involvement in children's education can lead to improved academic outcomes, better attendance, and increased motivation. Increased likelihood of behavioral problems, decreased school engagement, and poorer performance are not typically associated with family involvement. Reduced interest in learning, decreased social skills, and increased absenteeism are also not typically associated with family involvement. While the impact may vary depending on the specific circumstances, research suggests that family involvement can have a significant positive impact on academic achievement and school-related outcomes.

QUESTION 133

Answer: D

Explanation: While higher socioeconomic status is often associated with better family well-being, the relationship between the two is complex and influenced by many factors. Families with lower socioeconomic status may experience greater stress due to financial strain, limited access to resources, and reduced social support networks. However, some families with lower socioeconomic status may also demonstrate resilience and strength in the face of adversity. Factors such as access to resources, social support networks, and individual coping skills can influence the relationship between socioeconomic status and family well-being.

QUESTION 134

Answer: A

Explanation: Credit unions are non-profit organizations that are owned by their members and typically offer lower fees and interest rates compared to banks and other financial institutions. They prioritize personalized customer service and often have a community-focused approach. Insurance companies and payday loan centers typically do not offer savings accounts, while banks may charge higher fees and have stricter eligibility requirements.

QUESTION 135

This question is intentionally removed.

QUESTION 136

Answer: A

Explanation: Losing a job can be a stressful and challenging experience for individuals and families. However, there are several community resources that can help individuals like John during this difficult time. These resources include unemployment benefits, food banks, financial assistance programs, and job training programs. By accessing these resources, John can get the support he needs to meet his family's needs and overcome the challenges he is facing.

QUESTION 137

Answer: B

Explanation: The texture of materials is an important consideration when selecting furnishings for a home. Texture can affect the look and feel of a space, as well as the comfort of the furnishings. Materials with a soft texture, such as velvet or plush fabrics, may be more comfortable for seating, while materials with a rough texture, such as burlap or rough-woven fabrics, may be better suited for decorative accents.

QUESTION 138

Answer: D

Explanation: A debit card is linked to an individual's checking account and allows them to spend money they have available. A credit card, on the other hand, allows individuals to borrow money up to a certain limit and charges interest on the balance if not paid in full each month.

QUESTION 139

Answer: B

Explanation: Using a credit card to purchase a car is generally not a good idea because it can result in a high credit utilization ratio, which could harm Mark's credit score. Credit utilization is the amount of credit used compared to the amount of credit available, and a high credit utilization ratio can suggest that a person is overextended and may be a higher credit risk. Additionally, using a credit card to purchase a car may result in higher interest rates and fees than a traditional car loan.

QUESTION 140

Answer: B

Explanation: Lisa's decision-making strategy involves creating a decision matrix to evaluate the two cars based on objective factors such as price, fuel efficiency, carbon emissions, and safety ratings. This approach is rational as it involves a systematic and logical evaluation of options based on pre-determined criteria.

QUESTION 141

Answer: D

Explanation: All of the factors listed are important to consider before investing in a stock. The current price of the stock can give you an idea of whether it is undervalued or overvalued, while the company's financial statements and performance can tell you how well the company is doing financially. Additionally, you should consider the company's industry and competitors to see if there are any external factors that could affect the stock's performance.

QUESTION 142

Answer: B

Explanation: Seeking additional sources of income through a part-time job or side hustle is a strategy for adjusting resources to meet financial needs. Continuing to spend as usual, ignoring the problem, and borrowing money from family and friends may provide temporary relief but can lead to long-term financial difficulties.

QUESTION 143

Answer: B

Explanation: Sarah should prioritize paying off her student loans as part of her short-term financial management plan. This will help her reduce debt and improve her financial standing, which will give her more financial flexibility in the future. Investing in the stock market, saving for a down payment on a house, and planning for retirement are important long-term financial considerations that Sarah should address in the future, once she has taken care of her short-term financial obligations.

QUESTION 144

Answer: B

Explanation: Consulting with a financial advisor to create a retirement plan is a strategy for selecting resources to meet goals. Investing in high-risk stocks without considering their financial situation, ignoring the issue, and putting all of their savings into a single account without diversifying can lead to financial risks and uncertainty.

QUESTION 145

Answer: C

Explanation: While Javier signed a contract, he may still have legal options to cancel the membership if the gym is not fulfilling its obligations under the contract or if the contract contains unfair or illegal terms. Consulting with an attorney can help him understand his rights and options.

QUESTION 146

Answer: D

Explanation: When purchasing a new home, it is important to look for various safety features that ensure the safety of the occupants. This includes fire extinguishers, smoke alarms, and carbon monoxide detectors to detect and respond to potential fires or gas leaks. Adequate ventilation and insulation are important to prevent the buildup of mold, mildew, or other toxins that can affect indoor air quality. Well-maintained electrical wiring and plumbing can prevent electrocution or other safety hazards. Therefore, all of the above options are important safety features to consider when purchasing a new home.

QUESTION 147

Answer: C

Explanation: While thread color may affect the overall aesthetic of the garment, it does not impact the quality of the construction. Factors such as the type of fabric used, the skill level of the seamstress, and the type of stitch used are all important considerations in ensuring high-quality apparel construction.

QUESTION 148

Answer: A

Explanation: The durability of apparel construction is greatly influenced by the type of fabric used. Some fabrics, such as natural fibers like cotton or wool, are more durable than others. The color of the thread used, the style of the garment, and the time of day the garment was constructed are all relatively minor factors compared to the choice of fabric.

QUESTION 149

Answer: A

Explanation: Education level is a key factor that affects money management and financial planning throughout the life cycle. Research has shown that individuals with higher levels of education tend to have better financial literacy, make more informed financial decisions, and have greater access to financial resources. In contrast, individuals with lower levels of education may struggle with financial management and be more vulnerable to financial difficulties. While marital status, physical health, and religious affiliation can also impact financial planning, education level is considered a primary factor in determining financial literacy and stability.

QUESTION 150

Answer: B

Explanation: A credit score is a numerical rating that represents a person's creditworthiness. Lenders use credit scores to determine whether to approve a loan or credit application, and what interest rate to offer. A person's credit score is based on factors such as their payment history, credit utilization, length of credit history, types of credit used, and new credit inquiries.

QUESTION 151

Answer: C

Explanation: Consulting with a financial advisor to create a retirement plan and diversifying their investments is a strategy for selecting resources to meet goals. Putting all of their savings in a single investment account without diversifying, ignoring the issue, and investing all of their savings in high-risk stocks can lead to financial risks and uncertainty.

QUESTION 152

Answer: C

Explanation: Reading online reviews and ratings is a method for researching and comparing goods and services when making a consumer decision. Asking friends and family for their opinions can be biased and may not provide a comprehensive understanding of the product. Making a purchase without researching other options or only considering the price of the product can lead to poor purchasing decisions.

QUESTION 153

Answer: B

Explanation: When managing personal and work commitments, it can be easy to feel overwhelmed and like there aren't enough hours in the day. One strategy for effectively managing your time is to prioritize tasks based on their level of importance. This allows you to focus on the tasks that are most critical and make progress on them first, rather than getting bogged down in less important tasks.

QUESTION 154

Answer: A

Explanation: A food allergy is a reaction of the immune system to a specific food, which can cause a range of symptoms from mild (such as hives or itching) to severe (such as anaphylaxis). A food intolerance, on the other hand, is a digestive problem caused by the body's inability to digest a particular food, such as lactose intolerance. Both food allergies and food intolerances involve the body's response to a specific food, but they are caused by different mechanisms.

QUESTION 155

Answer: C

Explanation: Lighting is a design element that plays an important role in promoting safety and ease of movement in a space, especially for older adults. John and Sarah should consider adding task lighting near seating areas and walkways to improve visibility and reduce the risk of falls or accidents.

QUESTION 156

Answer: A

Explanation: "Sell-by" dates indicate the last day that the store should sell the product

QUESTION 157

Answer: D

Explanation: When planning a meal, it is important to consider nutritional balance and variety to ensure that all essential nutrients are included. Cost-effectiveness should also be considered to stay within a budget. Ease of preparation is important to save time and effort. All of these factors play a role in successful meal planning.

QUESTION 158

Answer: B

Explanation: Portion control is an important aspect of meal planning to ensure that the appropriate amount of food is consumed. Limiting calorie intake is crucial for weight management and overall health. Consistent serving sizes can also help with portion control, but the main purpose is to limit calorie intake.

QUESTION 159

Answer: A

Explanation: John is juggling a lot of commitments and feeling overwhelmed, so one potential resource that can help him manage his time more effectively is hiring a personal assistant to handle tasks. This could include things like managing his schedule, booking travel, or handling administrative tasks. By delegating some of these responsibilities to someone else, John may find that he has more time and energy to focus on his most important commitments.

QUESTION 160

Answer: C

Explanation: Lottery scams often involve sending fraudulent checks to victims, which are later found to be fake after they are deposited into the bank account. Reporting the check as fraudulent can prevent Sarah from being held liable for the deposited amount and help identify the scammers.

QUESTION 161

Answer: A

Explanation: Iron deficiency is characterized by a lack of sufficient iron in the body, which can lead to a decrease in the production of red blood cells and a subsequent decrease in oxygen transport to the tissues. This can result in fatigue and weakness, among other symptoms.

QUESTION 162

Answer: D

Explanation: Meal planning and preparation can promote healthy eating habits in multiple ways. By planning ahead, individuals can save time and effort required to make healthy meals, which can reduce the likelihood of choosing convenience foods that may be high in calories, sodium, and unhealthy fats. Meal planning can also help with portion control and calorie management, as well as increase variety and nutrient intake by including a range of fruits, vegetables, whole grains, lean proteins, and healthy fats.

QUESTION 163

Answer: D

Explanation: Wooden cutting boards are the best option for several reasons. First, they are softer than other materials, so they won't dull knives as quickly. Second, wood has natural antimicrobial properties, which means it can inhibit the growth of bacteria. Finally, wood is easy to clean and maintain.

QUESTION 164

Answer: A

Explanation: Cooking can cause the loss of certain nutrients in foods, particularly heat-sensitive nutrients such as vitamin C and B vitamins. However, cooking can also increase the availability of certain nutrients, such as lycopene in tomatoes, by breaking down cell walls and releasing the nutrient.

QUESTION 165

Answer: B

Explanation: Raw chicken can contain harmful bacteria such as Salmonella, which can cause food poisoning. The cutting board must be thoroughly cleaned with soap and water to prevent cross-contamination and eliminate any potential pathogens.

QUESTION 166

Answer: C

Explanation: Involving children in meal planning and preparation is an effective technique for establishing healthy eating habits in families. This can encourage children to try new foods and develop a sense of ownership and pride in the meals they help prepare. Strictly limiting all processed foods and snacks, encouraging children to clean their plates, and banning all sweets and desserts are not effective techniques and may lead to negative relationships with food and/or disordered eating habits.

QUESTION 167

Answer: C

Explanation: Olive oil is considered to be the healthiest type of oil to use for cooking. It is high in monounsaturated fats, which are good for heart health, and it also contains antioxidants that have been linked to a range of health benefits. Vegetable oil, on the other hand, is often highly processed and may contain unhealthy trans fats. Coconut oil is high in saturated fat, and while canola oil is a good choice, it doesn't have the same health benefits as olive oil.

QUESTION 168

Answer: B

Explanation: A foodborne illness is an illness caused by consuming contaminated food or water. Consuming undercooked chicken, which can be contaminated with harmful bacteria such as Salmonella or Campylobacter, is a common cause of foodborne illness.

QUESTION 169

Answer: C

Explanation: The USDA is responsible for regulating and inspecting meat, poultry, and egg products to ensure they are safe for consumption. The FDA is responsible for regulating other food products, while the EPA focuses on environmental protection. The CDC is responsible for disease prevention and control.

QUESTION 170

Answer: A

Explanation: The FDA is responsible for regulating and inspecting seafood products to ensure they are safe for consumption. The USDA regulates meat, poultry, and egg products, while the EPA focuses on environmental protection. The NOAA is responsible for managing ocean and coastal resources.

QUESTION 171

Answer: D

Explanation: Local health departments are responsible for enforcing food safety regulations in restaurants and grocery stores at the local level. The USDA and EPA are federal agencies that regulate food safety, while the CDC focuses on disease prevention and control.

QUESTION 172

Answer: A

Explanation: The FDA is responsible for regulating and inspecting bottled water to ensure it is safe for consumption. The EPA focuses on environmental protection, the USDA regulates meat, poultry, and egg products, and OSHA is responsible for workplace safety.

QUESTION 173

Answer: C

Explanation: The CDC is responsible for investigating foodborne illness outbreaks and coordinating with state and local health departments to prevent and control the spread of foodborne illnesses. The FDA and USDA regulate food safety, while the EPA focuses on environmental protection.

QUESTION 174

Answer: C

Explanation: Fresh fruits and vegetables should be stored in a cool, dry place with good air circulation. The best way to store them is in a plastic bag with holes punched in it, which allows for air circulation while keeping the produce from drying out too quickly.

QUESTION 175

Answer: B

Explanation: Preheating the oven is important to ensure even cooking of the food. If the oven is not preheated, the food may cook unevenly or take longer to cook.

QUESTION 176

Answer: D

Explanation: In this situation, Sarah attempted to modify the recipe by reducing the amount of sugar. However, she did not take into account how the sugar affects the texture of the cake, which resulted in a dry and crumbly cake. To successfully modify a recipe, it is important to understand how each ingredient affects the outcome and make adjustments accordingly.

QUESTION 177

Answer: C

Explanation: Knowledge of educational theory is the most important skill for Sarah to have in order to effectively teach diverse subjects in family and consumer sciences. This includes understanding how students learn, developing curriculum and lesson plans, and assessing student progress. While creativity and innovation can be helpful for developing engaging and interesting lessons, they do not replace the foundational knowledge of educational theory. Strong public speaking skills and proficiency in a foreign language are not directly relevant for teaching family and consumer sciences.

QUESTION 178

Answer: C

Explanation: Interning at a local hospital would be most beneficial for Katie to gain the necessary skills and knowledge for a career in nutrition and dietetics. This experience provides exposure to medical conditions, treatment plans, and dietary restrictions, which are all relevant for this field. While volunteering at a community center can be helpful for gaining experience working with diverse populations, it does not provide the same level of medical exposure as an internship at a hospital. Working as a cashier in a grocery store or in retail sales at a clothing store are not directly relevant for a career in nutrition and dietetics.

QUESTION 179

Answer: A

Explanation: Event planning falls under the category of hospitality and tourism, which is a major area of family and consumer sciences. Starting an event planning business can be an entrepreneurial opportunity for those interested in this field.

QUESTION 180

Answer: B

Explanation: Clothing and textiles is another major area of family and consumer sciences. Fashion designers create clothing, accessories, and footwear, using their knowledge of fabric, design, and sewing techniques.

QUESTION 181

Answer: C

Explanation: Engaging in unethical behavior is unacceptable in any workplace, and it is important to report such behavior to the appropriate authorities. Reporting the behavior to your supervisor or human resources department allows them to investigate the matter and take appropriate action to address the issue. Ignoring the behavior or engaging in the same behavior is not a responsible or ethical solution and could result in negative consequences for you and the organization.

QUESTION 182

Answer: B

Explanation: Sexual harassment is a serious issue that should be taken seriously by employers. Ignoring the complaint or dismissing it as unfounded can result in a hostile work environment and potential legal consequences for the organization. Investigating the complaint and taking appropriate action, such as disciplinary action or termination, if the complaint is substantiated, can help prevent future incidents and ensure that the workplace remains a safe and respectful environment for all employees.

QUESTION 183

This question is intentionally removed.

QUESTION 184

Answer: A

Explanation: When evaluating career options in Family and Consumer Sciences, personal interests and strengths should be considered. This includes considering what type of work the individual enjoys doing, as well as what they are good at. While the availability of job openings and income potential are important factors to consider, they should not be the sole deciding factor in choosing a career path. Potential for career growth and advancement is also important to consider, but should be balanced with personal interests and strengths.

QUESTION 185

Answer: B

Explanation: Providing excellent customer service is the most important factor in building strong customer/client relationships in a family and consumer sciences program. This involves listening to customers/clients, addressing their needs, and providing personalized solutions. Offering the lowest prices, a wide variety of services, or discounts may be helpful, but they do not necessarily contribute to building strong relationships if the customer/client feels undervalued or ignored.

QUESTION 186

Answer: A

Explanation: Communicating effectively is an example of a customer/client service skill. This involves using clear and concise language, active listening, and responding appropriately to customer/client needs. Cooking gourmet meals, sewing intricate designs, or conducting scientific experiments may be relevant skills for a family and consumer sciences program, but they do not necessarily contribute to effective customer/client service.

QUESTION 187

Answer: B

Explanation: To pursue a career in family and consumer sciences, it is important to have the necessary training, skills, experience, and aptitudes. While a Master's degree in education can be helpful, it is not always necessary for all positions in this field. On the other hand, certification in a specific area of family and consumer sciences is often a requirement for employment. This demonstrates a certain level of expertise and knowledge in a particular area, such as culinary arts or interior design. Experience in the hospitality industry can be beneficial, but it is not always a requirement for a career in family and consumer sciences. An aptitude for science and technology can also be useful, but it is not always necessary, depending on the specific career path.

QUESTION 188

Answer: C

Explanation: To teach family and consumer sciences in a high school setting, a Master's degree in education with a specialization in family and consumer sciences is typically required. This degree program provides specialized training in teaching methods, educational theory, and curriculum development specifically for family and consumer sciences.

QUESTION 189

Answer: C

Explanation: Family-style service is a meal service style where dishes are placed on large platters and passed around the table for guests to serve themselves. It is common in casual settings and promotes sharing and socializing.

QUESTION 190

Answer: C

Explanation: A formal table setting includes specific placements of dishes, silverware, glasses, and napkins. It is typically used in formal dining events such as weddings and formal dinners. Casual settings and picnic settings do not require a formal table setting, and buffet settings have a different layout.

QUESTION 191

Answer: B

Explanation: Effective communication skills are essential for success in a customer service role. Customer service representatives must be able to listen actively, understand customer needs, and respond in a clear and helpful manner. Good communication skills can help to build positive relationships with customers and enhance their experience.

QUESTION 192

Answer: A

Explanation: Dietitians are experts in the area of nutrition and wellness, and their primary focus is on helping clients develop healthy eating habits through meal planning and education.

QUESTION 193

Answer: A

Explanation: Child and family social workers provide support and assistance to families who may be experiencing crises, such as poverty, abuse, or neglect.

QUESTION 194

Answer: A

Explanation: Financial planners work with clients to develop strategies for managing their finances and achieving their financial goals, such as saving for retirement or paying for their children's education.

QUESTION 195

Answer: A

Explanation: FCCLA promotes civic engagement among students by providing opportunities for community service projects. Through these projects, students learn the value of giving back to their community and develop a sense of civic responsibility.

QUESTION 196

Answer: D

Explanation: Participation in FCCLA can benefit students in their future careers in a number of ways, including by providing networking opportunities with professionals in their field of interest, teaching students specific job skills, and providing opportunities for internships and job shadowing. By participating in FCCLA, students can gain valuable insights into their desired career paths and develop the skills and experience needed to succeed in those careers.

QUESTION 197

Answer: B

Explanation: The Fair Labor Standards Act (FLSA) requires employers to pay employees at least the minimum wage and overtime pay for hours worked over 40 hours in a workweek, unless the employee is exempt. To be exempt from these requirements, an employee must be paid on a salary basis and meet certain job duty tests, which typically involve performing executive, administrative, or professional duties. Being a manager or executive alone does not automatically exempt an employee from the FLSA's minimum wage and overtime pay requirements.

QUESTION 198

Answer: B

Explanation: The Family and Medical Leave Act (FMLA) requires covered employers to provide up to 12 weeks of unpaid leave to eligible employees for a serious health condition, the birth or adoption of a child, or to care for a family member with a serious health condition. Eligible employees must have worked for the employer for at least 12 months and have worked at least 1,250 hours during the 12-month period immediately preceding the start of the FMLA leave. Employers are required to provide job protection for employees on FMLA leave and must maintain their health benefits during the leave.

QUESTION 199

Answer: B

Explanation: A cover letter is a document that accompanies a resume when applying for a job. Its purpose is to express your interest in the job and highlight how your skills and experience match the job requirements. A cover letter should not simply summarize your work history and qualifications, nor should it be used to negotiate salary and benefits. Providing a list of references is also not typically included in a cover letter.

QUESTION 200

Answer: C

Explanation: During a job interview, it is common for the interviewer to ask questions that assess the candidate's problem-solving and conflict-resolution skills. Therefore, a about how the candidate would handle a difficult situation at work is more likely to be asked than a about the candidate's favorite color or whether they have been arrested. Questions about salary expectations may also be asked, but typically later in the interview process.

QUESTION 201

Answer: B

Explanation: Open-mindedness is a personal quality that involves being receptive to new ideas, perspectives, and feedback. In the workplace, open-mindedness can lead to creative problem-solving, effective teamwork, and personal growth.

QUESTION 202

Answer: B

Explanation: Collaboration and cooperation are important personal qualities that facilitate success in a team environment. When individuals work together effectively, they can share knowledge and skills, identify and solve problems, and achieve common goals.

QUESTION 203

Answer: C

Explanation: Effective delegation skills are important for success in project management. Delegating tasks to team members can help to reduce workload, optimize productivity, and ensure that all aspects of the project are completed on time and to the required standard.

QUESTION 204

Answer: C

Explanation: The demand for nutritionists and dietitians is expected to grow due to the increasing awareness of the role of food and nutrition in maintaining good health and preventing chronic diseases.

QUESTION 205

Answer: B

Explanation: The increasing demand for sustainable living practices has led to a growing need for professionals with expertise in sustainable design. By taking additional courses to gain this expertise, the recent graduate can enhance their skills and increase their chances of finding a job in their field.

QUESTION 206

Answer: D

Explanation: Starting a catering business in the food industry can provide significant opportunities for growth and profits, especially if the business offers unique and high-quality services. However, starting a business also involves risks and uncertainties, and the graduate should carefully consider all the factors before making a decision.

Printed in the USA
CPSIA information can be obtained
at www.ICGtesting.com
LVHW082250030624
782201LV00009B/486